THE
LOUIS D.
BRANDEIS
STORY

By the Author

THE
LOUIS D.
BRANDEIS
STORY

CATHERINE
OWENS
PEARE

Thomas Y. Crowell Company, New York

ACKNOWLEDGMENTS

I am indebted to many persons for their assistance in writing *The Louis D. Brandeis Story*. Members of Justice Brandeis's family were most generous with their time in helping me to understand my subject and present him accurately. A grandson, Frank B. Gilbert, Secretary of the New York City Landmarks Preservation Commission, read and commented upon much of the manuscript and gave me invaluable advice in compiling the quotations that appear at the beginning of each chapter. Others were Mrs. Pearl W. Von Allmen, Law Librarian, and faculty members of the School of Law, University of Louisville; Melvin I. Urofsky, Co-editor of the Brandeis Letters; and librarians at the Filson Club in Louisville, the Louisville Free Public Library, the Louisville *Courier-Journal,* the Missouri Historical Society in St. Louis, the St. Louis Public Library, the Boston Public Library, the Yale University Library, and the Zionist Archives and Library.

I should also like to thank the following for permission to quote from the published and unpublished works indicated: Abelard-Schuman, Limited, for *The Words of Justice Brandeis* edited by Solomon Goldman, 1953, copyright 1953 by Henry Schuman, Inc., published by Abelard-Schuman, Limited; Brandeis University for the text of the Epilogue; *Eastern and Western Review* for "An Analysis of Louis D. Brandeis" by Edgar Clifton Bross, August 1916; Harper & Row, Publishers, for *Trial and Error* by Chaim Weizmann, 1949; *Harvard Law Review* for "Mr. Justice Brandeis: A Centennial Memoir" by Paul A. Freund, March 1957, copyright 1957 by the Harvard Law Review Association; Houghton Mifflin Company for *Morning and Noon* by Dean Ache-

v

son, 1965; *Life* for "Justice Brandeis in Palestine" by William E. Smythe in the *American Review of Reviews,* June 1919. Princeton University Press for *Wilson: The New Freedom,* Vol. II, by Arthur S. Link, 1956; G. P. Putnam's Sons for *Arthur James Balfour* by Blanche E. C. Dugdale, 1937; Reynal & Co. for *Felix Frankfurter Reminisces: Recorded Talks with Dr. Harlan B. Phillips,* copyright © 1960 by Harlan B. Phillips, published by Reynal & Co.; *St. Louis Post-Dispatch* for the article by Charles G. Ross, June 19, 1927; Stackpole Books for *The Personal History of an American Ideal* by Alfred Lief, 1936; Syracuse University Press for *The Fall of a Railroad Empire* by Henry Lee Staples, 1947; University of Illinois Press for *Impatient Crusader* by Josephine Goldmark, 1953; University of Louisville for free use of their collection of Brandeis letters, manuscripts, and clipping books; University of Texas Press for *Viennese Revolution of 1848* by John Rath, 1957; The Viking Press, Inc., for *Brandeis: A Free Man's Life* by Alpheus Thomas Mason, 1946, and for *Pioneer's Progress* by Alvin Johnson, 1952; Zionist Organization of America for *Brandeis on Zionism* by Louis C. Brandeis, 1942.

The quotations that appear at the headings of Chapters 1, 2, 3, 4, 6, 7, 8, 12, and 13 are from opinions written by Justice Brandeis when he was a member of the Supreme Court and may be found in volumes of *U. S. Reports of Cases Argued and Adjudged in the Supreme Court of the United States.* Other quotations are from the letters, essays, and addresses of Justice Brandeis.

CHAPTER   1: Whitney v. California, 274 U.S. 357, page 375 (1927; a concurring opinion).

CHAPTER   2: Whitney v. California, 274 U.S. 357, page 375 (1927; concurring opinion).

CHAPTER   3: Olmstead v. United States, 277 U.S. 438, page 485 (1928; dissenting opinion).

CHAPTER 4: Whitney v. California, 274 U.S. 357, page 377 (1927; concurring opinion).

CHAPTER 5: Letter to Robert W. Bruère, February 25, 1922, quoted in *The Brandeis Reader,* edited by Ervin H. Pollack, page 220.

CHAPTER 6: Olmstead v. United States, 277 U.S. 438, page 478 (1928; dissenting opinion).

CHAPTER 7: Louis K. Liggett Co. v. Lee, 288 U.S. 517, page 580 (1933; dissenting opinion).

CHAPTER 8: New State Ice Co. v. Liebmann, 285 U.S. 262, page 311 (1932; dissenting opinion).

CHAPTER 9: "The Jewish Problem, How to Solve It," June, 1915. Reprinted in *Brandeis on Zionism,* by Louis D. Brandeis, page 28.

CHAPTER 10: *The Words of Justice Brandeis,* edited by Solomon Goldman, page 26.

CHAPTER 11: Speech delivered May 1923, quoted in *Brandeis on Zionism,* pages 127 and 129.

CHAPTER 12: Olmstead v. United States, 277 U.S. 438, page 479 (1928; dissenting opinion).

CHAPTER 13: New State Ice Co. v. Liebmann, 285 U.S. 262, page 311 (1932; dissenting opinion).

Contents

THE
LOUIS D.
BRANDEIS
STORY

Chapter 1

A SENSE OF FREEDOM

"Those who won our independence believed that the final end of the state was to make men free to develop their faculties. . . . They believed liberty to be the secret of happiness and courage to be the secret of liberty."

Two boys raced along Water Street, past the wharf where their father's freighter docked, past other wharfs. The riverfront swarmed with all sorts of people: merchants, mechanics, boatmen, stevedores loading and unloading cargoes, men, boys, whites, Negroes, Indians, shouting in every sort of accent— throaty Southern from Memphis and New Orleans, twangy Eastern from as far away as New York, German, French. Riverboats and railroads brought people to Louisville, Kentucky, from all over the world, traveling east and west, north and south. Louisville was a great river city on the southern side of the Ohio River.

Alfred and Louis Brandeis loved the Ohio River. It was half a mile wide at Louisville, deep, glistening silver and brown on some days and silver and blue on others. Streams fed it all the way from Pittsburgh, until the river boiled and churned over a limestone ledge that formed a shoal at Louisville. The Falls, people called it. The city had dug a canal alongside of the Falls to make the Ohio navigable at that point.

There were always steamboats and sailboats on the river, and the ferry that churned across to Jeffersonville, Indiana. Sometimes a river palace tied up at Louisville, gleaming white, driven by a huge side wheel. She would have brought passengers up the Mississippi and Ohio rivers, and would take others down. Sometimes long canoes skimmed over the surface.

Louis was not yet five, and he clung to his older brother's hand. It was always exciting to roam with Alfred and a little frightening, too. A horse and wagon rattled past them over the cobblestone street. Women in wide, tilting skirts, holding ruffled parasols over their heads, hurried along. The sun was getting low in the sky, turning the river to pink and the distant forest to purple.

"We had better go home," said Alfred. "We'll stop at Papa's store."

They turned up Third Street away from the river to the store of Brandeis and Crawford, grain and cotton merchants, but Adolph Brandeis had left. Then it was really dinnertime, and they had five blocks south and two over to reach their home on First Street. Panting and hot, the boys rushed to the door as their mother opened it.

"Hurry and wash and make yourselves tidy," said Frederika Brandeis.

They ran to their room, poured water from a pitcher into a large bowl, and sluiced their hands and faces. When they darted back to the dining room, they found the family already around the table: their two sisters, Fanny and Amy, aged ten and nine; Papa, a slender, gentle man with a long face and a neat moustache; Mother, sitting straight and prim, with her tiny waist, her face rather round, her eyes large and deep, and her long, dark hair parted in the middle and drawn back into a silken net. Uncle Lewis Dembitz was there, too. He was Mother's brother and quite a small man, with a bald head, a moustache and short beard.

"No talk of business at the dinner table," was Frederika Brandeis's rule as she presided over her family. Nobody minded. The Brandeises and their whole circle of friends were cultivated people who enjoyed new books, music, and world affairs.

Most of the talk at the dinner table and around the house was in German. Louis understood German, although he was still too young to grasp the ideas that were often discussed—a new play at the Lyceum Theatre or a concert at Mozart Hall. But he loved being in the midst of all the familiar voices, and he could catch some excitement from the sense of freedom which his family and their friends felt.

The adults were all refugees from oppression in Europe, keenly aware of their freedom of speech. Some of them had been political leaders. Some had been active in—or suspected of being active in—the Revolution of 1848 in Austria. The revolt for civil rights had failed, and that could have meant prison and death had they been arrested, even on suspicion. Louis' own family had not taken part, but they had been in danger of being suspected anyway. Because of that and because of the lack of economic opportunities in his native land, Louis Brandeis's father had come to America alone to find work and a place to live—eight years before Louis was born. In another few months he had sent for Louis' mother and twenty-five relatives. Meeting their ship in New York, he guided the group to Cincinnati, where many German-speaking people lived. Soon they moved on farther west to Indiana. By the time Louis was born on November 13, 1856, the family and many of their friends were established in Louisville, Kentucky. They had been well-to-do in Europe, and on the Brandeis table and sideboard stood pieces of fine china and sterling silver, in another room a piano, which they had been able to bring with them.

This evening there was more excitement than usual in the conversation. They were talking of slavery, secession, civil war. Far away on the eastern coast there had been fighting at Fort Sumter in South Carolina. President Lincoln had just declared it an insurrection, calling for seventy-five thousand volunteers to defend the Union.

"This means war at last," said one, and the others nodded.

All four children became animated, blurting out questions. "Will you be a soldier, Papa? Will you volunteer for President Lincoln?"

"Your father is nearly forty," their mother rebuked them. "He is too old to be a soldier."

This outbreak of war had been a long time

brewing. The Northern and Southern states had been growing farther and farther apart during the last twenty years, especially over the question of slavery. There were people all over the United States who wanted slavery abolished, but generally speaking, the abolitionist movement was strongest in the North. Those most fiercely opposed to outlawing slavery were the big plantation owners in the South. When Lincoln was elected the previous fall, it had been common talk to say, "Now there will be war." After the election, many Southern states began plans to secede from the Union. South Carolina had been first; then came Mississippi, Florida, Alabama, Georgia, Louisiana, and Texas.

What would Kentucky do? It was a big state, stretching along the southern side of the Ohio River for nearly five hundred miles. The people of Kentucky owned many slaves. In the city of Louisville alone there were five thousand, and the white population was seventy thousand. Across the river from Kentucky were Ohio, Indiana, and Illinois, all states with laws against slavery. On Kentucky's southern side lay Tennessee, a slave-owning state about to secede. Would Kentucky join the South or the North?

The Brandeises and Dembitzes were liberals who were against oppression of any sort. They knew from personal experience what it meant, and so quite naturally they abhorred slavery. In fact, the whole German population of Kentucky was opposed to slavery and secession. There were so many of them that their influence was tremendous.

The governor of Kentucky and the legislature decided that the solution would be for Kentucky to remain neutral. In wartime, feelings run so high that it is impossible to think calmly. "Kentucky is a Northern state!" "No, she is Southern!" Either of these remarks could bring on a fistfight, a rolling tussle in the dusty street. Men quarreled and fought; children fought because violence and fear filled the air all around them.

As Louis and Alfred Brandeis roamed about Louisville in the weeks that followed, they heard war talk everywhere. They heard men say they would slip over into Tennessee to the south and join the Confederate army. They heard others talk of crossing the Ohio into Indiana so that they could join the Union army. They wandered up and down fashionable Walnut and Chestnut streets, or hung around in front of the Galt House, Louisville's most elegant hotel. The war talk was the same everywhere, there, or in front of the Louisville Hotel on Main Street, where the wealthy planters stayed when they came into town, chewing big cigars, wearing wide-brimmed hats, and downing bourbon whiskey. The riverboatmen talked of the effect on

river trade, of the army patrol boats that were beginning to appear in the river, of trading with the
South or the North.

The boys watched military companies drilling
near the town, and they knew many of the men who
had joined them—the Louisville Battalion Guard,
the Louisville Light Guard, the Rough and Ready
Guards, the Kentucky Rifle Rangers—marching,
drilling, target practice. Before the end of April ten
companies were ready, camped just outside the city.

There were meetings all over town—Unionists,
Secessionists. The news that Fort Sumter had surrendered brought a big meeting of Secessionists to
the Louisville courthouse. The group drew up a petition with five hundred signatures: Kentucky must
secede! But while they met inside, another crowd
collected outside singing "The Star-spangled Ban-
ner" and shouting, "The Union! The Union forever!"
Doors were flung open; the two crowds leaped at
each other; and a bloody riot started.

Louis Brandeis was a gentle boy, growing up in
a gentle home. At five he did not understand why
there were suddenly so many soldiers marching in
town, so much anger in men's voices. He heard his
father say that two of his freighters had been sunk
near New Orleans. When he heard his father state,
"I shall sell wheat only to the Union and the Union
Army," it made him happy, and he thought he un-

derstood. His father knew how to be strong without being noisy about it.

By September 1861 the whole country was at war, and Kentucky became a battleground. The Louisville Home Guard patrolled the streets; there was a big recruiting station at Eighth and Main; and the courthouse was now a storage place for muskets, cartridges, and kegs of gunpowder. When the news broke that the Confederate army was invading Kentucky from the south, wild pandemonium spread through Louisville. The city would surely be attacked! The Confederate army was coming up the Ohio River valley, capturing river ports along the way. It had already seized Hickman, Columbus, and Paducah. Of course, it would try to take an important river port and railroad center like Louisville.

The next news was that General Grant was coming with Union troops to defend Kentucky against invasion. Troops in blue uniforms did come, rolling in on the Louisville and Nashville Railroad. Wild rumors spread that the Confederate army had reached Lebanon Junction, only forty miles to the south. Outfit after outfit of Union troops arrived, camping in every open space, the commanding officers taking quarters at the Galt House. Women met in the Masonic Temple to roll bandages, or they served coffee and food to the troops, and opened hospitals for the wounded. Every kind of business shut down as disorder spread. Soldiers got drunk and became rowdy. Children ran wild, begged, or stole.

Adolph Brandeis called his family together. He looked at all of them, especially the two boys.

"I am sending you all to New York City to visit the Wehles until conditions in Louisville quiet down a bit."

The Wehles were another large family group that had immigrated to the United States from Prague at the same time as the Brandeises and Dembitzes. They were relatives of Mrs. Brandeis. Her mother had been Fanny Wehle who married Siegmund Dembitz.

"Are you going with us, Papa?"

No, he had contracts with the federal government to find wheat for the Union army. He must remain at home and attend to that.

After the confusion of packing, Adolph Brandeis took his family to the railroad station and put them aboard the train that lumbered and panted in, spouting wood smoke from its stack and steam from around its wheels. None of the Brandeis children had ever really been anywhere before. Amy and Fanny, ten and eleven, did their best to seem adult in long full dresses just like their mother's. Alfred, eight, and Louis, six, hugged their father and then scrambled aboard to squash their noses against the train window, watching their father and the station and even Louisville disappear. They looked out of the window for hours at the rolling bluegrass country with its horse farms. Everybody in Kentucky owned horses and loved them, and many famous thoroughbreds came from there. At last the train reached the Blue Ridge Mountains, and the boys fell asleep—to awaken next day and discover they had been carried from one train to another. It took the Brandeises three days to reach their destination.

New York City turned out to be so big, it was amazing. The girls clung to each other; the boys clung to their mother's skirt; until someone hurried up to them and guided them to a waiting horse and carriage.

"We have just moved in to our new home on East Twenty-third Street," he told them as they rumbled and jounced over the cobblestone streets.

The streets were wide, crowded with carriages, hackney coaches, and wagons. The sidewalks were filled with jostling pedestrians. An omnibus drawn by a pair of horses rumbled past them. New York was really an island, nearly fourteen miles long. Its avenues running north and south seemed endless, lined with tall buildings on both sides.

The Wehle house was large, and there seemed to be enough room for everyone. In front of it, on the other side of Twenty-third Street, were open fields, and in the garden behind the house giant lilac bushes flourished.

Not until years later did Louis Brandeis sort out all of his Wehle relatives. There was great-uncle Gottlieb Wehle and his wife Eleanor and their several children. There was great-uncle Moritz Wehle and his wife and children. Whether the children were first, second, or third cousins was too much to figure out.

One thing was obvious right away. There was the same kind of freedom of speech here as in the Brandeises' home in Louisville, especially around the dinner table. Everybody enjoyed ideas and enjoyed exchanging them with one another. So far as Louis could tell, everyone was for President Lincoln and the Union and against slavery.

But Alfred and Louis were glad when they could return to Louisville. They jumped from the train into their father's arms, and as soon as the family buggy pulled up in front of their door, they ran into the house. But the boys and their two sisters became crestfallen when Adolph Brandeis told them they must remain close to the house. No roaming all over town and out into the country or along the Ohio River. Troops still occupied Louisville. Instead of being a center of trade, Louisville was now a center of army activities. Officers were quartered at the Galt; Union troops were recruited and drilled here;

Confederate prisoners captured farther south were brought to temporary prisons here until they could be transferred farther north. Had they not noticed the stacks of army supplies that blocked the sidewalks on Main Street?

And there was another danger. The Brandeises were Northern sympathizers, and Confederate feeling was running higher and growing more bitter every day. Something could happen to them because their father was helping the North. They *must* understand even though they were so young. The Confederate army to the south was strong; it could invade Kentucky again.

"You will be in school a good part of each day," Adolph Brandeis said to comfort them.

School to Louis Brandeis had been something mysterious that his sisters and Alfred did. Now, in the fall of 1862, he was old enough to go, too. Dressed in baggy knickers, stockings, and high-buttoned shoes, he walked with his mother to the home of Miss Wood who kept a private school for beginners. At home he had always been the youngest and often the favored one, but here all the children were the same age. He learned to wait his turn, to build, to write his name. Miss Wood was from England, and everything her children heard in class was said in excellent English. Louis Brandeis was American-born, and English must be his native tongue from

now on. In the future he would use German only occasionally with his mother and father, to be certain
of a meaning or to express his special love for them.

But Louis had scarcely become accustomed to
school when war panic again engulfed everyone.
The Confederate army was moving north into Kentucky for a second invasion. They were marching toward Lexington. Rumors move faster than any army.
The Confederates were here! They were there!
Then word got around that they were only ten miles
from Louisville. Actually they had captured Frankfort, the capital of Kentucky, only forty miles away,
and a Union army was marching to meet the invad-
ers.

Once more Adolph Brandeis acted for the safety
of his family. He bundled them all into a boat and
took them across the Ohio River to Indiana, to remain with friends until the danger had passed.

And the danger did pass. The two armies
clashed at Perryville, south of Frankfort, in a bloody,
tragic battle that turned out to be a stalemate. The
Confederate army retreated to Tennessee and never
invaded Kentucky again.

The Brandeises soon returned home, resuming
their usual activities. Mrs. Brandeis did wartime
community work with the other women in town.
One of her projects was to take baskets of food to a

fort, near the present site of the University of Louis-ville, where prisoners of the Union were held. Louis liked to get into the buggy and go with her when-ever she would allow it.

"If there is any food left in the baskets," he would remind her wistfully, "please remember that I am always hungry."

But school was his most important experience. After only a year with Miss Wood he was ready for the private school where his brother had gone ahead of him—the German and English Academy on Gray Street at the corner of Second, just one block up and two over from his home. Adolph Brandeis had meant what he said about keeping them close to home as long as the Union army occupied Louis-ville.

German-speaking people are clannish anyway, and at the German and English Academy Louis Brandeis could cherish his German heritage, all the while learning in English, and understand that his German-speaking background was a contribution to American culture, one that would melt together with many others.

The Brandeises did not attend any synagogue, and the children did not attend any religious school. They never made a special issue of the fact that they were Jewish. The Brandeises, Dembitzes, and

Wehles were as liberal about religion as about everything else, believing that there is one God for everyone.

"I do not believe that sins can be expiated by going to divine service and observing this or that formula; I believe that only goodness and truth and conduct that is humane and self-sacrificing towards those who need us can bring God nearer to us, and that our errors can only be atoned for by acting in a more kindly spirit. Love, virtue, and truth are the foundation upon which the education of the child must be based," was how Frederika Brandeis explained it.

Louis Brandeis was a natural scholar, and to him learning was its own excuse for being. He learned around the house by listening to adult conversations; he learned at school—penmanship, grammar in both English and German, geometry, algebra, history, chemistry, French, Latin, drawing, gymnastics. The academy's courses were stiff, but his grades were usually excellent. He did so well that at least once a teacher wrote a note on his report card that he deserved "special commendation for conduct and industry." The more he studied and understood, the more he could communicate with the world around him. Yet he seldom had to go beyond the circle of his family and their friends to be alive in a world of great ideas that stimulated his imagination.

Of all his relatives outside the immediate family, Uncle Lewis Dembitz was the most inspiring. The bespectacled little man who weighed only about a hundred pounds was one of the most respected citizens in Louisville. He and his sister Frederika, Louis' mother, had grown up in the little town of Zirke, Poland, where their father was a doctor. Their mother had died while they were still children, and they were sent to live with their uncle, Moritz Wehle, in Prague. Their grandparents lived in Prague, too. They were grown—Frederika nineteen and Lewis fifteen—by the time the Revolution of 1848 forced the families into exile in America.

Coming to America so young, Lewis Dembitz had the chance to become fluent in English and to study American law in Cincinnati. Along with the rest of the huge family he moved on to Madison, Indiana, and finally settled in Louisville, to become a successful attorney, a political leader, a delegate to the Republican National Convention that nominated Lincoln, and eventually, assistant city attorney of Louisville. His office was in Court Place and his home on the west side of First Street, between Gray and Chestnut, was just across the street and a block away from Louis' house.

Naturally Uncle Lewis came to his sister's home often. Louis loved being at the table when Uncle Lewis was there, because Lewis Dembitz knew so much about so many things. He could usually excite everyone with some original idea.

As Louis Brandeis grew older, he sought out his Uncle Lewis more and more, sometimes passing hours in his law office. He began to realize that a lawyer with creative imagination could make law work for mankind. Uncle Lewis talked of improving the method of collecting city taxes; he wanted the election laws improved and would eventually draft a new election law for Louisville providing for a secret ballot. Laws were all written by men for the benefit of men, and they must be improved by men for their greater benefit. Louis Brandeis very soon knew that he wanted his own career to be law. He admired his uncle so profoundly that he changed his own name from Louis David Brandeis to Louis Dembitz Brandeis.

Uncle Lewis, his mother and father, his sisters and brother, were nearly all his world, especially in wartime when there were so many things a boy could not do and so many places he could not go. But he and Alfred managed to entertain themselves. By the third year of war they had learned to live in a city ruled by an army. At night they could ring doorbells in the neighborhood and disappear into the dark before anyone came to the door. Up and down their street lived girls they could tease. One of their particular joys was to stuff a dummy with straw and stand it where it would startle the maid. Silently, clinging to each other in a corner, they would await her shriek of terror: "An escaped prisoner of war! Beware!"

Their father could not keep them away from the war; the army brought it right to their front door by laying temporary railroad tracks down First Street to transport supplies. Of course, there were opportunities for the boys in the neighborhood to pilfer from the army's stores.

Alfred and Louis got hold of some flaring powder, and while they were experimenting with it the powder ignited. In an instant it singed and blackened their faces and left them with no eyebrows or lashes. Confused, skin stinging, they leaped up, screaming, and bolted into the house for help. There was no serious physical injury, but they did have to answer a few questions. Where did they get the flaring powder? What did they think they were going to do with it? "We were celebrating the Fourth of July!" they wailed.

Wars always end eventually. The people of Louisville knew the Civil War was reaching its conclusion when generals like Ulysses S. Grant and William T. Sherman met at the Galt House to plan final strategies. So many officers and top personnel came and went that everyone sensed big plans in the air. Soon news filtered back of Sherman's victories in

Georgia and the Carolinas. Then, in April 1865, Lee surrendered at Appomattox.

Louisville went wild when the telegraph wires tick-ticked the news that the war was over. Flags and bunting went up everywhere; shouting, cheering crowds surged through the streets. Riverboat horns and whistles honked and screeched. There was no holding Alfred and Louis as they ran up First Street to the center of town, struggling through the crowds. It was over! Father had said they could go anywhere when the war was over. As darkness fell every window in the city was ablaze with light, the Galt Hotel a beacon against the sky. The boys peered through a window and saw ladies and gentlemen dancing, laughing, crying.

Exhausted, they found their way home at last, and no one seemed to mind what they had done. Everyone was too happy. Their own family was dancing, laughing, and crying, too.

The joy lasted only a few days, until the telegraph wires ticked out the news that President Lincoln had been assassinated. Then the city of Louisville draped itself in black; offices and schools closed; and the crowds were quiet and gentle. A procession three miles long moved through the streets in Lincoln's memory—every dignitary and officeholder, wounded soldiers, mounts with portraits of Lincoln and his generals.

Gradually life returned to normal. The army of occupation marched away. Adolph Brandeis and other merchants talked of resuming trade with the South, of sending their freighters down the Ohio and Mississippi rivers to New Orleans once more.

Louis and his brother could roam where they would after school and on holidays—up and down the Ohio, out into the countryside. Or the two boys could mount horses and gallop over the rolling hills and meadows, through pastures and stretches of wood, scaring up quail, leaping rail fences, then reining their horses around to gallop past the race track or to whiz past groves of ash trees and tobacco fields, and scarcely notice the dark blue morning glories. Louis loved riding horseback. Astride a swift mount he felt a renewed sense of freedom.

And he felt mature, way beyond his years, mature and ambitious to get on with his schooling so that he could begin the study of law.

Chapter 2
WIDER HORIZONS

"Order cannot be secured merely through fear of punishment for its infraction . . . the path of safety lies in the opportunity to discuss freely supposed grievances and proposed remedies; and the fitting remedy for evil counsels is good ones."

Louis Brandeis entered Louisville Male High School in 1868, shortly before his twelfth birthday. He had grown taller by then. His blue eyes were noticeably large and expressive and set well apart. He had the high, wide forehead of a scholar, a prominent but straight nose, and a rounded chin. His straight black hair grew rather long and down over his ears and highlighted his fine olive skin. Now that he had begun to mature, it was obvious that he would always have a gentle and gracious disposition.

High school met in the same building as the Fifth Ward public school at the corner of Ninth and Chestnut. There he sat in classes with Louisville boys he had never known before, boys from every part of the city whose backgrounds were neither German nor Jewish. Some came from families who had lived in Kentucky since log-cabin days, owners of tobacco plantations or thoroughbred horse farms. Others were the sons of riverboatmen, of employees in town, or of merchants like Louis' own father. Most of them were Christian of some Protestant denomination. They all got on together without much difficulty, but there were many he never seemed to know well, especially those of the oldest Kentucky families.

But he would never be dependent upon the companionship and approval of others. His true happiness was in his studies, more so than ever before, because he now had such a clear sense of direction. He progressed swiftly with his French, Latin, chemistry, and algebra; moved on to other new subjects; brought home the same excellent grades. He particularly liked opportunities to rise and recite in class; a lawyer must be at home on his feet and speak well on the spur of the moment. He was already a member of the Websterian Debating Society, a group that met for the pure pleasure of arguing the pros and cons of political issues.

Louis Brandeis was taking his place with the rest of his family as cultural leaders of Louisville. Not only did they love to attend debates by the Websterians, but other gatherings that shared ideas on art, new books, and music. Music was one of their particular pleasures, and every child in the family had a turn at music lessons. Fanny was showing real talent and often entertained them at the piano in the evening.

When Louis chose the violin as his instrument, Fanny said, "I will practice with you every Monday and Thursday and sometimes on Saturday." Louis was growing closer to both of his sisters, now that he had reached his teens and was over his dislike of girls.

He arrived with great confidence at the studio of Louis H. Hast for his first music lesson. Music was interesting; his whole family had an ear for it; others in his family had musical talent; so he must have talent, too. When Mr. Hast settled the violin under his own chin and drew the bow across the strings, a tone came out liquid, clear, and rich. Then he handed the instrument to Louis, showed him how to hold it, how to position his hands and wrists. Louis drew the bow across the strings, and a harsh squawk emerged.

"Don't be discouraged," said Mr. Hast. "Now we will begin our lessons."

Louis took his violin seriously. He appeared regularly for lessons and practiced in between, sometimes with Fanny. He got rid of the squawk and learned to produce clear tones, until finally he could play well enough to be in Mr. Hast's orchestra. "Henry Watterson and I played the overture to *Zampa* in Mr. Hast's orchestra," he told a friend after about three years of music lessons.

But that certain brilliant something did not occur in his playing, and Mr. Hast knew it never would. "You are not a musician," he told Louis in the kindliest possible voice. "I advise you to give up music and devote yourself to your other studies."

The advice was hard to accept. But after a talk with his mother and father, Louis did decide to stop his lessons.

Discovering a field for which he did not qualify was a helpful experience. It made him take a good look at himself and realize that he had limitations like everyone else. In his schoolwork his progress was amazing. He finished his high school subjects in two years and was ready to graduate at fourteen, the youngest in his graduating group.

His graduation was a great day for the Brandeis family. Feeling stiff and self-conscious in his new suit, Louis sat on the platform awaiting his turn to receive his diploma, saying his speech over and over to himself. But when the moment arrived and he rose to accept the scroll, he opened his mouth to speak, and there was no sound at all. He had lost his voice in the tension and excitement. The confidence he had gained in reciting and debating vanished, and all he could do was to bow politely, swallow hard, and sit down. Hot and embarrassed, he left the stage at the end of the ceremony and wandered out into the schoolyard. Suddenly he saw another student, bigger, just enough older to have lured a girl away from him some months ago. How did it start? They were on the ground, fighting, beating each other with their fists, rolling over and over, until a crowd gathered and separated them. Choking, sobbing, dirty, his clothing awry, Louis let Alfred and the others take him home.

The warm Kentucky summer—riding, walking, waiting for a floating palace to come up the Ohio— soothed feelings and healed spirits. So did his family, especially now that he was becoming old enough to share in the problems and concerns that confronted his parents.

Adolph Brandeis was doing some hard thinking about the times in which they lived. The Civil War had been over for five years. The Thirteenth Amendment to the Constitution had abolished slavery, and in 1868 General Grant had been elected to the Presidency. There had been prosperity for a while, due largely to postwar rebuilding. Elegance had returned to their own city—to such hotels as the Galt House and the Louisville Hotel, to its concert halls and to the theater where famous actors came to perform. People promenaded at the racetrack in expensive clothing or took carriage rides through town and out into the country on Sunday afternoon.

But the boom was tapering off. Louis' father could see it in his ledger books. President Grant's financial policies were not helpful, either. The economic situation bore careful watching.

Louis Brandeis began classes at the University of the Public Schools in Louisville in September. Since he lived at home, it really seemed like a continuation of high school. His mother was in St. Louis at the time, and so he wrote to her about it:

Louisville
September 7, 1870

My dear darling Ma:
    As I can't write to you tomorrow morning, I use my time tonight to write a few lines and congratulate my dear Ma on her wedding day,

*the first one I have not been with you. I hope
you are having a splendid time. I know Alfred
is. We are all a little sick (home sick but not
sick of home) today but otherwise are very well.*

*Today the regular lessons began and there
was yawning done in our room which would
have done justice to Pa. I study only French,
Latin, Chemistry, German, Algebra, Composi-
tion, Trigonometry: Mathematics and Languages being the principal studies.*

*We went out riding with Aunt Rosa on the
river road yesterday. Aunt Lotti and Mrs. Knef-
ler were here this afternoon. . . . Pa is at the
Opera House meeting tonight. Fanny is going
to the Prussian meeting tomorrow afternoon.
. . . Amy is troubling me awful as she wants to
write, so goodbye. Hoping you will soon be
back to your*

> *Loving son*
> *Louis*

She did soon come back, in plenty of time for
the Christmas season, a carnival time for everyone of
every creed. Louisville was even gayer at Christmas
than at racing time. The Brandeises and Dembitzes
could hold open house, ready with brimming bowls
of eggnog for the parade of friends and well-wishers
who called.

Louis studied at the university for two years—reading, reading, consuming books away beyond the requirements of his courses—until he received a gold medal for "pre-eminence in all his studies." By that time everyone—family, friends, classmates—knew Louis Dembitz Brandeis to be an exceptional person. He wasn't a grind, certainly, and not a bookworm hiding away in books for some unhappy reason. Books were a genuine joy. But in his sensitive face, especially in his large, deep eyes, there was an expression that made it seem as though he saw more and saw farther than others. When a book had given him a new experience, he would lift his head and look off into the distance while his imagination raced on with ideas of his own.

By 1872 he knew as much about American politics and economics as his parents. The economic situation had grown worse during President Grant's administration. There had been one bad slump in the security markets, and Adolph Brandeis foresaw others. He could tell by the way the wholesale prices of grain were behaving. Speculators were building railroads too fast, which added to the danger. Inflation was increasing.

"Instead of waiting to be wiped out when the crash comes," Adolph Brandeis told his family, "Mr. Crawford and I have decided to close down our business until times are better. Meanwhile we will

all take a nice long vacation in Europe." He thought
it would be best to sell their house and buy or build
another when they returned.

Europe! A trip to Europe! Everybody's eyes
were bright and misty. The children were no longer
children. They were all grown and old enough to be
on their own over there. Fanny, the oldest, was
twenty-one; Amy, twenty; Alfred, eighteen; and
Louis, sixteen. They could scarcely contain themselves, all talking at once, laughing, asking a million
questions. What would they take? What clothing?
Oh, they'd have to go shopping.

But all four young people began to realize very
quickly that they were simply excited about a new
adventure and that the trip meant something much
deeper for their parents. They had been born in
America—three of them in Louisville—and so they
had no memories of any other world. It had never
before quite occurred to them that Adolph Brandeis
and Frederika Dembitz were profoundly homesick
for anywhere else. They began to pay attention to
the history of Austria, the cities of Vienna and
Prague, the Revolution of 1848 that had driven their
parents, the Dembitzes, Wehles, and many more into
exile.

Austria in the heart of Europe had been a big
and powerful empire in olden times, governed by a

succession of absolute monarchs known as the Habsburgs. When Louis' parents were small children, the country where they were born included not only Austria but what later became Czechoslovakia, Hungary, Rumania, part of Poland, and northern Italy. It was a major power in European politics. Under Emperor Francis I and his minister of foreign affairs, Prince Clemens von Metternich, the Austro-Hungarian empire controlled the balance of power in the whole European continent. The emperor and Prince Metternich created a police state within the country with spies, arrests without trial, complete repression of human liberties. There was widespread poverty among the lower classes, because they were denied so many opportunities.

Louis' father had been born in Prague, in the Czech region of the Austro-Hungarian empire in 1822; his mother had been born in the same city seven years later. They could remember the hardships under the old monarchy, and they could recall the unrest that gathered steadily during their youth. Monarchies were being overthrown in other countries, and people were winning constitutions that guaranteed freedom of expression. A revolution in France for "liberty, equality, fraternity," had overthrown the ruling family there. In spite of tight censorship, news of these revolutions and reforms reached the subjects of the Habsburgs. The country was filled with unrest that increased and spread until it burst into revolution in 1848.

"The March Twelfth Revolution!" the Brandeises liked to call it.

It had happened in Vienna since that was the seat of the government. Francis I had died in 1835, and the new monarch, his son Ferdinand, was mentally incompetent, had epileptic fits, and let the ruthless Metternich rule with an iron hand. The revolution developed under the leadership of the educated classes—doctors, lawyers, teachers, university students. On the twelfth of March, 1848, they sent a petition containing thousands of signatures to the emperor. The petition demanded a more representative government, an end of secret courts and unfair trials, religious toleration, personal liberty, better education for more people.

The city was turbulent with excitement. Throngs filled the streets; thousands of them were students from the University of Vienna. They waited all day for the emperor's reply. Toward evening a rumor began to circulate that the emperor had rejected most of the terms of the petition, that he was calling out troops to disperse the crowds. Noise and excitement mounted.

That night the students decided to march on the Landhaus, where the assembly was to meet to consider the petition. And in the morning they were seething and milling outside the building. This was insurrection, the government knew, and it was happening all over Austria.

Two doctors from the General Hospital, Adolph Fischhof and Joseph Goldmark, were in the crowd. They were popular with the young men, especially with the medical students. When Fischhof shouted, "Gentlemen! Listen!" they boosted him up on their shoulders to make a speech. It was a significant day, he told them. The Austrian Estates (assembly) were meeting inside the building to consider the will of the people. "Hail to the united peoples of Austria! Hail to freedom!"

The crowd cheered and applauded. Other speakers followed.

"But none spoke like Dr. Goldmark," Adolph and Frederika wanted their children to realize.

Dr. Goldmark had climbed up on a balcony and urged the people to act. "We have had enough talk among ourselves. Now is the time to get the Estates to act." He wanted them to make the assembly go to the emperor and demand the dismissal of Metternich. The crowd roared approval, pressed forward to the great double door of the Landhaus, forced it open, and surged inside, Dr. Fischhof at their head. A marshal tried to stop them with promises of action.

Outside the mass of students still pressed forward, not knowing what was happening inside. A rumor began to spread: Fischhof had been arrested! Anger rose. "Give us a constitution! Down with Metternich!"

Just then shots rang out nearby and triggered the crowd into a rioting mob, fighting, clubbing, pillaging, wrecking doors and windows. Soldiers appeared and fired upon the mob, beat them with their gun barrels, swung right and left with swords. Violent fighting broke out all over the city, far more than the soldiers could cope with. In another few hours Metternich had resigned his post and fled from the country, and within two days the people of Austria-Hungary had been promised freedom of speech, a representative government, and a new constitution.

"Dr. Goldmark became a captain of the Academic Legion and president of the Student Committee." Yes, Louis and Alfred and their sisters knew that Dr. Goldmark had become an outstanding leader in the liberal movement in Austria.

But the liberal movement lasted only a few months. Sections of the empire, such as Hungary and Bohemia where the Czechs lived, struggled to separate themselves and become independent countries. Liberals became divided among themselves because they were of so many different backgrounds.

The monarchy saw its chance. The sickly Ferdinand abdicated in favor of his nephew Francis Joseph. He was competent and ruthless. The new constitution, freedom of speech, and all the other civil liberties, came to an end, and liberal leaders had to flee from the country before the secret police could find them.

When Dr. Goldmark learned that he had been charged with treason, he slipped over the border into Germany and then to Switzerland. In another few months he was in New York. Now in 1872 Dr. Goldmark and his family lived in Second Place, Brooklyn, New York, and owned a successful factory on the Gowanus Canal, for making percussion caps.

Louis Brandeis had been so young on his first visit to New York that he could not remember Dr. Goldmark clearly. Now he was eager to meet this courageous and brilliant man.

His head was spinning with other ideas, too—of seeing London, Paris, Vienna, and Prague. He and Alfred would do some real mountain climbing in Switzerland. He even talked with his father about remaining in Vienna to attend the university—the same university where the students had gathered for their march upon the Landhaus.

Louis and his family spent several weeks in New York before sailing. During that time he did meet Dr. Goldmark, and he sensed the older man's greatness at once. He made friends quickly with the doctor's fifteen-year-old son, Henry Goldmark, and played with his six-year-old daughter, Alice. Conversations with Dr. Goldmark added to the atmosphere of excited anticipation. And soon Louis began to feel that in a way he, too, was returning home to Austria. The political situation had eased in the last twenty-four years. His parents would now be in no danger of arrest.

Their ship, the S. S. *Adriatic,* a White Star liner, sailed from Jersey City on August tenth. Once aboard, Louis and Alfred lived in a world of their own, learning to know the feel of a deck moving beneath their feet, learning new terms: salon, topside, below, fore, aft, port, and starboard. They had studied the Gulf Stream in school, and it became real on this voyage. Temperatures at sea were mild for a while, but when the ship left the Gulf Stream, the color of the water changed, and the air grew suddenly chilly. Their ship put in at Liverpool seven days later.

Liverpool, the English countryside, London, and even France were all part of a happy holiday, but not until they crossed into Austria and finally stepped from the train at the railway station in Vienna did the Brandeises begin to show their deepest emotions. They were *here!*

Once settled in their hotel rooms, Louis and

Alfred took leave of the others as soon as possible, and set out to explore.

Vienna was the storybook city they had expected. Its buildings were ornate, full of decorations and carvings. Statues of angels, heroes, and sometimes devils stood on the corners of rooftops or supported ceilings on their shoulders. The oldest part of town, on the southern side of the Danube River, had been a medieval city, encircled by a high wall and a moat. The moat was filled in now, and the wall crumbling away, as the city had spread out and built on all sides and across the river. In the center of old Vienna stood the famous Cathedral of St. Stephen, its slender, cone-shaped tower rising high above everything else in the city. At noon the bells of St. Stephen's began to chime happily and soon church-bells all over the city were pealing the midday. It sounded like a musical celebration. Vienna was famous for its music. Mozart had lived here. So had Beethoven.

Louis was particularly interested in the University of Vienna, where the students had begun their civil-liberties march. He wanted to enroll in the *Gymnasium,* or secondary school, in Vienna, but he did not have enough credits. He did have a chance during the coming winter to attend some special courses at the university.

They all enjoyed Vienna—the cafés and coffee-houses, the shops, old friends, concerts, and theaters —prattling in German until all four young people became fluent in the language. But nothing compared to their holiday in Prague. Prague was more than 150 miles north of Vienna; it was the capital of Bohemia where the Czech people lived. This ancient city, where Good King Wenceslaus had once reigned, made Louis Brandeis realize how very old this part of the world really was. It, too, had been a medieval town with its ancient castle, wall, and moat; and like Vienna it had spread out beyond its old walls, to both sides of the River Moldau. The moat was now a boulevard. Its buildings were ornate, decorated with statues, and wherever Louis looked there seemed to be square towers rising.

Prague was truly home to Louis' parents. Their emotions ran deep, and they grew tense as they found the streets they knew so well. "Here, here was our house, where your Uncle Lewis Dembitz and I lived, where the Wehles lived." This was one of the oldest Jewish sections in Europe. "Look at that old synagogue. It goes back to the thirteenth century." "And there, just over there, so near the Wehles' house was the cotton mill where your father was working when I met him." In the old Jewish graveyard they found stones for many Brandeises, Dembitzes, and Wehles going back many generations. Some had been scholars; many, landowners.

Whenever Adolph and Frederika presented their four grown children to anyone, their eyes glistened and their voices were husky. They had left Europe when they were only engaged to be married, and now they were a family of six.

They went on with their holiday in the spring, to Italy to visit the cities of Venice, Genoa, and Milan. But the heat and humidity of Italy began to oppress them, and Amy came down with typhoid fever. As soon as she was able to travel, they set out for the cooler, drier air of Switzerland.

For Louis and Alfred, it meant that at last they could do the mountain climbing they had planned. The sweeping steep mountains of Switzerland were a joy to the eye, glistening white against a brilliant blue sky. And Swiss cottages with their sharp gabled roofs stood near swift mountain streams or against the side of a hill, looking down into a lake.

The two young men donned their gear—heavy cleated shoes, walking sticks with spiked points, rope—and set out. At first they strode along, but suddenly had to stop to catch their breath. The altitude! But they were young; it did not take them long to be on their way again.

On one of their hikes they decided to find the

source of the River Inn. As they started up the steep ascent, it was great! It was fine! It was also exhausting. At last they flung themselves on the ground to rest. Alfred had far more endurance than Louis, and in a few moments he sat up completely restored. "Let's explore the River Adda, too, while we are at it!" he said to his brother.

Louis was still flat on the ground, panting. "I don't see why I should have to find the source of every damned river in Europe!" he gasped.

All of these travel experiences were part of his education. Climbing a mountain, going to a concert, walking along a handsome boulevard, attending lectures at a university—all added to his growth. He could feel it happening inside of himself. He decided he wanted to gain still more from Europe by enrolling in a school—the Annen-Realschule in the city of Dresden, Germany.

But Amy was still too ill to travel. "We must remain in Switzerland with her," Louis' father told him. "You will have to go to Dresden by yourself, if that is what you want to do."

It definitely was.

Meanwhile Alfred announced he had had enough of Europe and wanted to go home and start his life.

Adolph Brandeis had kept in touch with affairs in America. The financial collapse he had foreseen was occurring. The panic of 1873 had resulted from too much speculation and unwise government policies. Banks failed; businesses went bankrupt; unemployment increased. Mr. Brandeis and his wife agreed that they might as well stay in Europe until the American economy began to improve. Did Alfred still want to go home? Yes, he did. He would have difficulty finding work, with no experience and not enough education, his father pointed out. Alfred decided to study for a while at Washington University in St. Louis, and his father let him go.

Louis set out for Dresden soon after, traveling by himself for the first time in his life—in a foreign country and to a strange city. The whole experience was glamorous, from the European-style train, with the aisle down one side of the coach and compartments that seated six passengers, to the rolling green hills of eastern Germany.

Dresden was the capital of the ancient kingdom of Saxony. Louis caught sight of it from the train window, in the wide valley of the Elbe River. Its weathered copper roofs gleamed in the sun, and it bristled with spires and towers.

As he stepped off the train to the platform, he knew himself to be an adult. He could claim his luggage, summon a carriage, and find his hotel with no trouble at all. Then off on foot he went at once to learn his way around still another city and locate his school. The pattern was familiar by now: a very old city with its oldest part planned around an ancient castle on the southern bank of the Elbe, the newer city spread all around it and across the river. Dresden was compact; he could see most of it in a few hours. There were excursion boats, plying up and down the Elbe, which gave him a twinge of homesickness for the Ohio. He found a big city park, the Grosser Garten, that he planned to explore some day —especially when he caught a glimpse of the bridle path.

The Annen-Realschule was a long stone building, three stories high, set in a wide flat area. It looked cold and forbidding. An acquaintance who was to have introduced Louis to the school principal failed to appear, and Louis was not sure he could find the courage to go in by himself. He walked completely around the building—then around again. Not until he had circled the school a third time did he approach the big double front door. But once inside his strength seemed to return, and he entered the office of the rector, Herr Job. He had come to enroll, he explained.

"You must have a birth certificate and proof of vaccination," the rector told him.

In a gentle but firm manner, not unlike his father, Louis Brandeis replied, "The fact that I am here is proof of my birth, and you may look at my arm for evidence that I was vaccinated."

There was something about the young man, standing quietly at attention, with his black hair, blue eyes, and sensitive face that the rector could not resist. But he raised one more problem: Brandeis would have to take an entrance examination.

Brandeis protested; he had understood that the school would waive the examination. Apparently there had been some misunderstanding on this point, but the candidate did not leave, and he did not give up. He went on speaking quietly and effectively about his qualifications for admission, until he won his way in without the examination.

Annen-Realschule was Louis' first boarding-school experience—bare rooms, cots, plain furniture, strange young men for roommates. Germany was a land of discipline, he learned quickly. He was accustomed to making most of his own decisions, but here his days were laid out for him with strict rules about when he could and could not leave the school, long hours for classes and study. Instructors held themselves stiffly erect and spoke in a brusque manner. The boys must be just as formal—and respectful.

Because he was so self-reliant, Louis Brandeis was able to accept German discipline for nearly two years. He was in Dresden to study, and that part he loved. The teaching and grading were similar to the German and American school he had attended in Louisville. He carried twelve subjects at a time. The French, Latin, and German he had had before, but much of the mathematics was new, and his science courses—mineralogy, chemistry, physics—were a real experience. They taught him something that he hadn't quite realized before: that he could examine an array of facts, compare them, combine them in different ways, and arrive at a wholly new and original idea. Deduction! It meant taking known facts, sitting back in his chair, mulling them over, reflecting about them, and realizing in his own imagination a future fact, something that was probably so, that would be discovered some day.

"At Dresden I learned how to think," he told a friend years later.

Annen-Realschule was not all study and discipline, though. There were free hours to take a boat trip or explore the old castle. In the Grosser Garten he could ride horseback, visit the museum, the zoo, and the lakes, until the snows and deep freeze of winter left him only walking as a recreation.

One evening he had been visiting a family in town and returned to the school after dark. But he had forgotten his key. He walked around to the window of his room and whistled up to his roommate to come down and let him in. A staff member heard the commotion, ordered him to the office, and gave him a severe talking to—for *whistling!*

Louis Brandeis had been at the school nearly two years and in Europe nearly three. He had begun to realize that he did not belong in Europe. He was neither German nor Austrian, but an American—a Kentuckian. In Kentucky a man could make his own decisions; he could be an individual, rove through endless countryside, or whistle if he chose.

When letters from his family told him they were preparing to return to the United States, he wrote back, "I am coming with you."

Teachers and students at Annen-Realschule had learned to love and admire him—particularly his fine scholarship. To be sure he realized it, they presented him with, "A prize awarded out of the Heymann Endowment to the honor student, Louis Dembitz Brandeis, for industry and good behavior by the faculty of the Annen-Realschule, Dresden, March 19, 1875. M. Job, Rector." Permitted to choose his own gift, Louis Brandeis asked for a book on Greek art.

He was with his family once more on May 5, 1875, to go aboard a ship at Le Havre, France, bound for America. As the ship put out to sea and the French coast began to disappear, he knew he was taking home a treasure of experiences that would help him for the rest of his life. He had visited places he had known only in storybooks before:

his parents' homeland, baroque cities. He had climbed breathtaking mountains and had completed intensive studies in Dresden. Most important of all, he had met people of talent and ability. Many of the young American men whom he had met studying abroad would always be his friends. By the time the ship reached New York, these new friends—who would soon return home themselves—began to seem like the most important thing he had found in Europe.

Chapter 3

HARVARD LAW SCHOOL

"Our government is the potent, the omnipresent teacher. For good or for ill, it teaches the whole people by its example. Crime is contagious. If the government becomes a law-breaker, it breeds contempt for law."

One of the many valuable friendships Louis Brandeis made during his three years in Europe was with Ephraim Emerton, who was about five years older than himself. Emerton had graduated from Harvard College and was now studying history at Leipzig, Germany, only fifty miles from Dresden. He loved to talk about Harvard and intended to return there to teach. Knowing Emerton made Brandeis think seriously about going to Harvard Law School.

He still intended to follow in the steps of his Uncle Lewis Dembitz and study law, and he had known for a long time that the Harvard Law School was one of the best in the country. En route home across the Atlantic, he and his family had time to discuss the matter thoroughly. Adolph Brandeis must begin all over again in business. Louis must remember that money would be scarce and that Harvard was expensive. But Louis was so intent upon the idea that when they reached New York, his family interrupted their journey home to take the train to Boston. There they visited with friends in Brookline while Louis went to Cambridge.

Cambridge was just across the Charles River from Boston, he discovered. It was another town on the bank of another lovely river. But it was not built around a medieval castle; there were no crumbling walls or filled-in moat. Yet Cambridge had every bit as much charm as Vienna or Dresden; its personality was entirely its own. The heart of this town was the oldest college in America.

Louis walked along Massachusetts Avenue to Harvard Square, catching glimpses of big white colonial homes down this tree-shaded street or that. He turned right along the second side of Harvard Yard, with its green lawns and brick buildings. By May 1875 the college, now a university, had grown way beyond its original space.

The law school was in Dane Hall abutting directly on Harvard Square, another red-brick building, two stories, with windows so tall he could tell that the ceilings inside must be very high indeed. He did not have to walk around this school three times, seeking the courage to enter. Louis Brandeis felt *native* here—and qualified. Fortified with his two intensive years of study at Dresden, he mounted the four steps and walked between the Greek columns and through the door—to be interviewed and have his scholarship examined.

Having applied for admission in the fall, he strode out of Dane Hall to the street. He must walk and walk and walk to work off his excitement—from Harvard Square to the Charles River and along its curving bank. Perhaps he could do some boating here. On Brattle Street stood the house where Henry Wadsworth Longfellow was still living and writing, and in the nearby town of Concord the aging Ralph Waldo Emerson had his home. So did Bronson Alcott, the educator and father of Louisa May Alcott. There on the other side of the Charles was Boston, capital of abolition, built up the slopes of Beacon Hill. He could walk across the bridge to Boston.

Now before him he had the whole summer—to return home with his parents and sisters, enjoy Kentucky after three years of absence, spend hours with his brother Alfred, who had returned to Louisville to go into business with his father.

The whole Brandeis family was glad to be home. The air was warm and fragrant with roses, and everyone seemed relaxed and easy of pace. The city was still trying to recover from its first Kentucky Derby at Churchill Downs. Everyone wanted to talk about it and about the splendid champion, Aristides, who had won.

Louis enjoyed his reunion with Kentucky, riding horseback over the countryside with Alfred, hiking along the Ohio, whistling if he chose. But when he had been at home only a few weeks, he realized that Kentucky was no longer the answer to his future. He had caught a vision of a farther horizon: Cambridge, Boston, New England—a region where people were dignified and sophisticated, yet free and progressive. He had had no feeling there that being a Jew made any difference. It did make a difference in Kentucky, in a subtle sort of way. In many parts of Europe it made a terrible difference. His parents and grandparents had had to live in a ghetto in Prague.

New England must be the place, then, to complete his education. Alfred had agreed to lend him two hundred dollars, so that it would be possible.

Even though the law school had not assigned him any summer work, Louis Brandeis felt that he must prepare himself. He could not wait until fall to begin studying. Quite naturally he turned to his Uncle Lewis for advice and learned that James Kent's *Commentaries on American Law* was an important work. Four big thick volumes! That was nothing; he took the whole set back to his room and began to work. So far as he could tell, Kent covered all the aspects of law. There were laws governing people and property, towns and states and nations. He really felt as though he had been over a lot of ground when he finished Kent.

All summer he read law, talked law with Uncle Lewis, and sometimes sat around with Alfred and Otto Wehle, a second cousin just beginning his law practice in Louisville. They argued happily and with great authority about how law ought to be taught. Should a law student sit in a lawyer's office and read? Or should he attend classes at a university? And what was the value of mock—or make-believe —trials?

In the fall Brandeis discovered that Harvard

Law School had considered all of these questions. He discovered as well that his curriculum took a very different approach from Kent's *Commentaries.* During his first year he would study the law of torts. (A tort is a private wrong done by one person to another.) His other first-year subjects would include real property, contracts, and criminal law.

Eventually he could look forward to a course in constitutional law. The United States Constitution? He had read a lot about it. His family often discussed it around the dinner table. It had been amended three times since the Civil War: to abolish slavery, to make the Negro a citizen, and to give him the right to vote. Constitutional law could be a career in itself.

Cambridge really had what he was looking for! And he had what Cambridge was looking for, too. There were about two hundred young men in his class. Without meaning to, and without realizing it, he became outstanding almost at once. The other students noticed him, because he was polished and polite in his manner. The youngest in his class, he was tall, slender, and so handsome that some of the men felt a little envious. But they were attracted to him at the same time.

"Mr. Brandeis had hardly taken his seat in our classroom before his remarkable talents were discovered and his claim to immediate distinction allowed," said one of his classmates years later. "The pleasant voice of that youthful student, his exact and choice language, his keen intellectual face, his lithe figure, his dark, yet handsome aspect, and finally the unaffected suavity of his manner that had in it something of the polish of the Old World. Intellect, refinement, an alert and receptive spirit, were written all over his attractive personality."

His alert spirit could scarcely contain itself when he first visited the library. In that solemn, high-ceilinged room the walls were lined with more than fifteen thousand volumes.

He lived at 29 Thayer Hall in the Yard.

The chief problem confronting him was how to earn enough money to remain at Harvard and to repay Alfred's loan. He was so brilliant that students came to him for help with their work, and he was able to earn money as a private tutor. All this was in addition to a heavy schedule of study.

The dean of the Harvard Law School believed in learning from experience. His students must learn theory from textbooks, but they must also study law in action. That is, they must study actual cases that had occurred in courtrooms: the arguments on both sides and the decisions. Textbooks were not enough. They must do research and argue cases themselves. Dean Christopher Columbus Langdell was noted all over the United States for the fine preparation he and his staff of teachers gave the young men who came to the Harvard Law School.

Most of the young men who studied there agreed with their dean that experience was the best teacher. And so for many years it had been the tradition to have law clubs. Members met in the evening and held court—a moot, or make-believe, court. One student acted as attorney for the defendant, the accused, and another for the plaintiff. They did as much work as they would for a real case and went through all the procedures of a real trial. Other members presided as justices. Sometimes the club invited an experienced lawyer to come in and preside.

Louis Brandeis was elected early to the oldest and most important law club at the school, the Pow Wow. Its membership list is full of the names of famous alumni. Whenever he pled a case before the Superior Court of the Pow Wow, it was the most important case of his life. He dug and searched and prepared. Because he had learned how to think, and because he had a crystal-clear mind, he could be counted on for an original approach. The Pow Wow Club was a great incentive. It wasn't make-believe to him; it was as real as any courtroom.

He wrote long letters home about the Pow Wow trials—to his brother and sisters, his parents, to Otto Wehle and Uncle Lewis. And he wrote about his instructors, his classmates, and friends in Cambridge and Boston. He especially enjoyed telling Otto Wehle and Uncle Lewis about his studies. Brandeis was beginning to think legally, to enjoy talking law, to live with it and love it.

But he went at his studies and his tutoring so intensely that first year at Harvard that his eyes began to pain him. Sometimes his vision blurred, and his eyes became bloodshot. "That is eyestrain," some of his classmates told him. The only lighting they had in those days either in the library or their rooms was from the dancing flames of gas jets, almost as bad as reading by candles. He went on with his reading anyway.

"Better ease off a bit, Brandeis," one student or another said.

He'd do that when he returned to Louisville for the summer.

When his first year ended and he reached Kentucky, he walked into a happy turmoil of planning for his older sister's wedding. The bridegroom was Charles Nagel of St. Louis.

"I met Charlie at Washington University in St. Louis," Alfred explained.

The Nagel family had immigrated to the United States about the same time as the Brandeises and Wehles. They had settled in Texas, which was wild country then. It became a really dangerous place to be during the Civil War, since the Nagels were op-

posed to slavery. They had to flee into Mexico in a
horse and buggy in 1863, when Charles was fourteen. There they hid in an abandoned warehouse
from Mexican outlaws. Managing at last to get out
of Mexico by boat, they came to New York, and because they spoke only German, found their way to
Cincinnati and then St. Louis.

Charles Nagel didn't know a word of English
when he entered St. Louis Central High School, but
he graduated valedictorian. He now had his own
law office in St. Louis. When he came to Louisville
to marry Fanny Brandeis, he was a strikingly handsome man, six feet four inches tall, with blond hair
and blue eyes, who towered above everyone, especially five-foot Uncle Lewis.

In spite of the happy stir of having this interesting man in the house, Frederika and Adolph Brandeis noticed Louis' red-rimmed eyes, his run-down
condition, and sallow color.

"You have been overworking, Louis. You need
rest and recreation."

He knew they were right and did go horseback
riding and hiking with Alfred until some of his glow
came back. But there was so much studying to be
done. He intended to read law in Otto Wehle's office
while he was home. When his parents heard that,
they threw up their hands. "You are an adult now,
Louis; you must show better judgment." But he

didn't listen to their pleadings. Books were something he could not resist. After poring over the fine print of Otto Wehle's lawbooks in the daytime, he read great classics in the evening—Sir Thomas More's poetry, Plato's *Republic*.

At last it happened. The print blurred; the room blurred; the world turned a shadowy gray. Was he going blind?

"We shall see," said Adolph Brandeis sadly.

He sent Louis to a specialist in Cincinnati, who told him that his vision was all right, but the muscles of his eyes were so badly strained that he *must* stop reading. He would have to give up his study of law, at least for the time being.

What would the world be like without vision? The Ohio River would never turn from brown to green to pink in the sunset. In Cambridge there would be no red buildings among green shade trees, no Boston church spires against a blue sky. But what would the world be like without law? Give up law? Law would not give him up. Give up? Not on one man's opinion. A lawyer ought to know better than that.

Against all advice Louis Brandeis returned to Cambridge in the fall. This was the second year when the work should be much more interesting than the first, especially the course in constitutional law.

He did have the good sense, however, to go to a Boston doctor. Result? The same advice all over again. "Stop using your eyes; you should probably give up your study of law." Further, he was badly run-down and must have regular recreation. Brandeis decided that he would plan to take some exercise at a gymnasium, but he would not give up his studies. A long letter to his father drew a long reply, telling him to consult an eye specialist in New York.

"It won't hurt you to read less and think more," said the New York doctor.

Back in Harvard, Brandeis thought about the comment. He probably had been stuffing himself like a starving man at a banquet. But how could he stop reading and still study law? Perhaps he could persuade one or another of his classmates to read to him.

As it turned out, several of them were willing to read assignments aloud while he sat with his eyes closed, taking it in through his ears. The method worked, and it gave his memory some sharp training.

Out of it grew a life-long friendship with one of his readers, Samuel Dennis Warren, Jr. Sam Warren was twenty-five, about four years older than Brandeis. His family were well-to-do—the owners of big paper mills—and prominent in Boston. Sam enjoyed the study of law as much as Brandeis. Studying together gave them a chance to think together. The more they thought together, the deeper their friendship grew. Warren introduced Louis to his parents, brothers, and sisters, and to other outstanding old families in Boston. There were the Lowells—writers, professors—all of them learned and cultivated. He became acquainted with James T. Field, the publisher.

By then Louis Brandeis had become friendly with many Harvard professors and instructors. Ephraim Emerton had returned from Europe during Brandeis's second year to begin teaching at Harvard. Another was Frank William Taussig who later taught economics. Taussig's father had been born in Prague. During the Revolution of 1848 he and his brother James had been students at the University of Prague and active in the rebellion. Like so many others, they and their families had fled when the revolution failed.

"My father, William Taussig, is quite prominent in St. Louis," said Mr. Taussig. "He was chairman of the committee that directed the building of the Eads Bridge across the Mississippi River at that point. My uncle, James Taussig, is a lawyer in St. Louis."

St. Louis? Louis Brandeis's sister had moved to St. Louis with her husband, Charles Nagel. The teacher nodded; Uncle James knew Charles Nagel.

Louis Brandeis did not realize that these people

whom he found so delightful were just as attracted to him. They saw so much promise in this brilliant, subtle young man! And his quiet conservative manner appealed to the most proper of Bostonians.

He was really something of a phenomenon at the Harvard Law School. Only twenty when he completed his two years, he achieved the highest grades in the history of the school—straight A's—or an average of 97.

"This poses a problem," said the dean. "You see, Brandeis, you are too young to graduate. You must be twenty-one."

His entire class was upset about it. Brandeis was their valedictorian! Yet the whole thing hung fire until graduation day, when the Harvard overseers (trustees) voted at the last minute to suspend the rule. Louis Brandeis could take his place with the two hundred men who were graduating.

Chapter 4
ST. LOUIS

"Those who won our independence by revolution were not cowards. They did not fear political change. They did not exalt order at the cost of liberty. . . . If there be time to expose through discussion the falsehood and fallacies, to avert the evil by the processes of education, the remedy to be applied is more speech, not enforced silence."

There was a certain amount of danger in returning to Kentucky by train in 1877. Railroad employees were beginning to strike and demonstrate for higher wages and better working conditions. Wages had been low in many fields since the crash of 1873. A number of railroads had gone bankrupt. Now four years later when the major railroads declared a 10 percent cut in wages, trouble started in earnest. Strikes, riots, and protest marches began to break out in one city after another. Rioters sometimes tore up tracks and burned switches. There were not yet any unions strong enough to speak for the workers, and so the police simply fought the strikers.

Louis Brandeis reached home without mishap, but he found his family disturbed and worried about the unrest throughout the country. By July it was at its worst. When trainmen of the Baltimore and Ohio struck, all freight trains stopped, and that affected his father's wholesale business. Federal troops were called out to put down the strike, making matters worse. Then the Erie Railroad struck. Its unskilled laborers wanted their pay raised to a dollar and a half a day; skilled men like brakemen and switchmen wanted two dollars. There were bloody riots in Pittsburgh, Philadelphia, Baltimore, and Buffalo. Mobs of unemployed joined the strikers.

For a while it looked as though Louisville would be spared, but at last the Louisville and Nash-

ville Railroad men went out, too. Disturbances occurred all over town. One afternoon when Louis and
his brother returned home for dinner, they found a
front window smashed. Demonstrations were contagious; they grew bigger, better organized. A shouting, rowdy parade roared through town from the
Nashville depot along the north side of Broadway to
Third Street, breaking street lights and windows as
they went. The police couldn't cope with the situation, and so the people of Louisville decided to deal
with it themselves.

Louis, Alfred, their father, and a large group of
leading men gathered in the courthouse for a conference. They decided to become vigilantes. Far into
the night the planning went on, so late in fact that
Louis and others slept on tables in the jury rooms.

Louis' duty would be to patrol the streets several nights a week, gun in hand. When he picked up
the long, heavy weapon that he must carry on his
shoulder, he realized he had no idea how to handle
a gun. What would happen if he had to use it? And
why was he carrying it at all? A man who picked up
a gun must have killing in mind. What had this to
do with law?

His patrol didn't last long. At the end of July
the president of the Louisville and Nashville Railroad promised to restore the wage cuts, and the
strike ended. There were no more riots in Louisville.

They died down in other cities, too. But the labor movement was definitely underway in America.

Louis Brandeis laid thoughts of labor problems aside for the time being and returned to his own affairs. His first concern was to become self-supporting. Two years at Harvard had proved that he could make it on his own. He had done it with almost no financial help from his father. In fact, by working hard and living modestly, he had been able to pay back his brother's loan and have fifteen hundred dollars left over.

He had learned something else: that the man who works perpetually isn't free. He had almost killed himself on a treadmill of work during those two years at law school; he must not live his whole life that way. Some day, he dreamed, he would be independent—*and free.* Someday he would have so much money ahead that he would be *free* to do whatever kind of work he pleased.

What would his next step be?

Otto Wehle wasn't available for conference, because he was busy courting Louis' sister Amy. Soon they were planning their wedding.

But many others were available with advice and help in that big, close family. Louis' brother-in-law, Charles Nagel, wanted him to come to St. Louis. The idea of living near his sister Fanny was tempting; he missed her often. His being in St. Louis would probably be a comfort to her, too, since her health wasn't always good. But by the end of the summer Louis had decided to return to Harvard for a third year of study.

Well, then, said Nagel, could he not come to St. Louis the *next* year? "If you come here next year, I expect, of course, that you would come into our office." That was the law firm of d'Arcy & Nagel. Louis didn't want to commit himself so far ahead, and he didn't answer the letter.

"Dear Louis," Charlie Nagel wrote again. "Your silence makes Fan feel somewhat uneasy. She fears that your eyes are bad. I hope that they are not and think that my letter may have caused you some trouble. Do not let it. If anything is awkwardly expressed, believe me now that everything was meant for the best.

"I thought I might touch upon the subject mentioned without in any way creating an awkward situation. Do not forget that no one more than I concedes your chances! Gladstone the student was not yet premier and might never have been; so I tell Fan that you may never be Chief Justice; although I do think that your chances for excellence are fine. . . ."

Brandeis was grateful to Charlie Nagel for being so understanding. Somehow, accepting a favored spot in the law office of his sister's husband did not seem like the next logical step to independence. And so he went back to Cambridge to put an extra polish on his legal training.

Very soon after his return he was appointed a proctor, a kind of monitor, to supervise other students, particularly when they were taking exams. Proctoring and tutoring solved his financial situation, and he knew how to be frugal. A man simply had to spend less than he earned, and that was how he intended to get ahead. He rather liked plain living.

For this third year, he and Warren roomed together in Boston, high up on Beacon Hill in back of the Warren family home. It brought him closer to the Warren family and all their friends. Among them was Oliver Wendell Holmes, Jr., whose law firm, Shattuck, Holmes & Munroe, Sam Warren had joined. Holmes, son of the writer and poet, was in his late thirties, tall, slender, regal in bearing, with blue eyes and a moustache, one of *the* attorneys of Boston.

Probably the most extraordinary experience—a true high point—of this last year at Harvard was meeting Ralph Waldo Emerson, poet, teacher, philosopher. The invitation had come from Professor James Bradley Thayer of the Law School:

> *"Mr. R. W. Emerson is to be at my home on Tuesday evening and will read a lecture to a*

*few of our friends on 'Education.' If it would in-
terest you to see him and hear him I wish you
would come in at 8 o'c. He is, you know, old
now, and perhaps one who had not seen him before would not quite understand the great
charm that he and all he says have for his
friends. . . ."*

Old? Emerson? Never. He may have been seventy-five by the calendar when Brandeis met him, but
his mind was keen and alert. Emerson's face with its
prominent nose and luminous brown eyes had a
youthful innocence about it, but at the same time it
showed wisdom. He had been pastor of the Old
North Church in Boston for several years and after
that had lectured at Harvard. Never blessed with
very much money, Emerson knew how to live simply with plain possessions. It wasn't what he said on
education so much as what he radiated—part of the
glow of this wonderful region—a love of gentleness
and universal freedom.

Brandeis felt deeply in tune with New England,
Boston and Cambridge in particular. But there were
so many brilliant and accomplished lawyers there
that it was no place for a lad of twenty-one to make
a beginning. Another letter from Charlie Nagel
made him think of St. Louis once more. There was a
job open in the law office of James Taussig, Frank

W. Taussig's "Uncle James." It was a salaried position as law clerk, but one in which Nagel thought
his brother-in-law would have a lot of personal freedom to work in his own way. "I think you can take
this position and preserve every kind of independence. The present incumbent does. And if upon
trial you do not like the place, you need merely
leave it," Nagel wrote. Louis decided to accept.

Because Louis Brandeis was a sensitive,
thoughtful person, he knew that every decision he
made about his life affected many others—his parents in particular. They really wanted him back in
Louisville. But Louisville now seemed provincial. In
Boston he had acquired a taste for complete freedom
of the mind. His sister Amy would remain in Louisville now that she had married Otto Wehle, and his
brother Alfred, who was going to marry Jennie
Taussig—the daughter of James Taussig's brother,
William—planned to stay there also. But even
though Louis knew his parents could scarcely consider themselves deserted with two of their children
remaining in Louisville, he went through a certain
amount of anguish over the decision anyway.

He wrote his mother a long letter explaining
why he thought St. Louis held more opportunity for
him than Louisville. When he did not hear at once,
he wrote a second letter:

Dearest Mamma:
Since writing this letter, I have doubted some-
what whether I was right in the course I pur-
sued in this matter. If after reading the letter
you think I was wrong, I most humbly beg your
pardon.

Lovingly,
Louis

His letters had been in English, as they always were. Both of his parents wrote to him in German, as they always did.

"I never felt prouder and happier about my boy," his mother said, among many other fine thoughts.

Adolph Brandeis wasn't even surprised at his son's decision to go to St. Louis. He had watched Louis outgrow his hometown. "You are so young, you can afford to risk something," he advised.

Another attraction that St. Louis held for Brandeis was the fact that a Law School classmate of his, Walter Bond Douglas, was now living there and practicing law. They had kept in touch. Douglas would become a justice of the Missouri Circuit Court and his son James M. Douglas would one day be a member of the Supreme Court of Missouri. Wal-

ter Douglas and Louis Brandeis were destined to be
friends for the rest of their days.

Louis Brandeis's plans were all set. Except that
they weren't. His head began to spin; he felt hot
and feverish, sweaty; then such a severe chill took
hold of him that his teeth chattered. Wretched,
wretched! The doctor had no difficulty recognizing
malaria. But how long would that take? How long
would he be laid up? He ought to set out for St.
Louis right away. His new job wouldn't wait forever.

Not until November 1878 did he finally reach
St. Louis. As the train rumbled across the half-mile-
wide Mississippi River, St. Louis looked like a long
black smudge against the sky, soft coal smoke bil-
lowing up from tall factory chimneys. St. Louis was
larger than Boston, about half the size of New York
City, and it had nearly twenty miles of riverfront. It
was booming, growing, prospering, a railway center
for trains from the east going to California, Kansas,
Texas, and Tennessee. And it was a trading center
for wheat, cotton, hogs, and manufactured goods.
Wealthy beer barons had their plants and expensive
homes here. Brandeis knew he would hear a lot of
German spoken, because something like a third of
the population of St. Louis was German, some American-born, some immigrants like his own parents.
Once across the river the train descended into a tun-

nel that ran underneath Washington Street and then emerged into Union Depot.

There was a room waiting for him in his sister's home at 2044 Lafayette Avenue, a big ample house near Lafayette Park. The park was a stretch of woodland in the heart of the city, which made St. Louis seem less smoky and sooty.

"Mr. Taussig has held your job open for you," the Nagels assured him.

The office where he would be a law clerk at fifty dollars a month was at 505 Chestnut Street, between Fifth and Sixth streets. It was near the river, in the oldest part of town, just behind the Court House. Chestnut Street ran toward the river, and the Court House stood on the north side of Fourth Street facing the Mississippi. In those days the spire on top of its dome dominated the whole city. Today the breath-taking Gateway Arch stands directly in front of the Old Court House, many times taller.

Louis Brandeis could not practice law when he arrived, because he had not yet been admitted to the bar. But his references and training were both so fine that he was admitted to the Missouri bar less than a month after his arrival. James Taussig had agreed that once admitted to practice he could spend some of his time developing his own law practice. And so, with his usual drive, he had letterheads printed—Louis D. Brandeis, Attorney at Law, 505 Chestnut Street, St. Louis, Missouri—and eagerly awaited clients. One actually came to him in December. A lady dropped in at his office for legal advice that took a matter of minutes to give. Fee: five dollars. A few more such bits and pieces came his way, and that was about it.

Shortly after the first of the year he pled his first case in court. He took infinite pains with his preparation, just as he had when he argued before the Superior Court of the Pow Wow. But the men in this courtroom were not his fellow law students, and the case he argued had never been tried before. As a matter of fact, it wasn't his case, but one of Mr. Taussig's brother's. Brandeis spoke for only about three minutes—with a dry mouth, a trembling voice, and a feeling of exhaustion when he sat down.

He just wasn't clicking in St. Louis, and he knew it. The kind of law he really wanted to practice required thought and careful analysis—and originality. His work so far had been too routine.

A recurrence of malaria added to his discouragement. If he took a walk through Lafayette Park —along the lake where swans glided by, or under the tall trees—it didn't raise his spirits. The air seemed too humid and heavy. Letters from his parents and brother and from his other sister, Amy Wehle, were not enough. Except for Walter Bond

Douglas and a few others, he could find very little stimulating conversation. People here preferred big parties—usually dances—and conversing interminably about polite nothings.

"You are so young, you can afford to risk something," his father had said.

Well, he had risked it. Now what?

A letter from Sam Warren in Boston wiped out his depression.

"Come back to Boston," Warren pleaded, "and we will form a law partnership of our own." He added that a law magazine in Boston needed an editor. The salary would tide Brandeis over until their firm acquired enough clients to become self-supporting. Brandeis began to think hard about the idea. Warren wrote him again; Holmes had told him there was a definite lack of real talent at the Boston bar.

On the thirtieth of May 1879, Brandeis sent Warren a long letter. It seemed like a good thing, he said. The salary as editor would certainly help, and he liked writing and the literary side of law. But how much of his time would the magazine take up? "I wish to become known as a practicing lawyer." And there was the further problem of overtaxing his vision: "My eyes, though quite strong again, allowing me to work practically the whole day and as much as is ordinarily required in a lawyer's practice, must be still carefully used. . . . I wish to postpone for a little while my final answer as to starting a firm together. . . ."

While he disciplined himself to make a slow and careful decision, he knew he was being drawn back to Boston and all the intellectual people he would mingle with there. At last he did write to Warren, accepting the invitation to form a law partnership. Charles Nagel was sorry to see him go, and so was Walter Bond Douglas, but they both admitted that Brandeis was making a wise decision. Boston held much more for him.

Chapter 5

WARREN & BRANDEIS, COUNSELORS AT LAW

"Refuse to accept as inevitable any evil in business (e.g., irregularity of employment). Refuse to tolerate any immoral practice (e.g., espionage). . . . Seek for betterment within the broad lines of existing institutions. Do so by attacking evil in situ; *and proceed from the individual to the general. Remember that progress is necessarily slow; that remedies are necessarily tentative."*

When Sam Warren and Louis Brandeis clasped hands in partnership in their new offices, two flights up at 60–62 Devonshire Street, Boston, they were beginning a professional association that would last for ten years. Their friendship would last the rest of their lives.

They'd make out well, they were sure, with hard work. Warren had what Brandeis called a "bulldog perseverance," and Brandeis was orderly and imaginative. They could be candid with one another, sit down and think out loud together until a problem was solved.

Both men were single. Warren lived with his family in Mount Vernon Street, and Brandeis found board and lodging with a Mrs. Smith at 21 Joy Street. All three addresses were in the heart of old Boston, near the State House, the courthouse, and Boston Common. Devonshire Street is east of the State House, running north and south; Joy Street is on top of Beacon Hill, bounding the west side of the State House; Mount Vernon crosses Joy.

Boston was alive and bustling. From the State House on top of the hill, its gold dome dominating the whole city, down the hill to the wide green expanse of the Common, Louis Brandeis could walk and fill himself with the vitality of this city and its brisk sea air. He could stride along Beacon Street on one side of the Common or along Boylston Street on the other, and turn toward the Charles River. He was going to enjoy that river; he was going canoeing on it. Beyond the Charles was Cambridge and Harvard.

The idea that he had left home for good, that Boston was to be his home, made him feel a little desolate and homesick for a while.

"Dearest Mother," he wrote from his room in Joy Street on Sunday, July 20, 1879. "When I received your letter and those of the others, it seems to me as if I were a fool to have settled here so far away, instead of staying with you and enjoying you and your love. Of course one can live anywhere, but there is also ambition to be satisfied. . . . And so I think that I shall be happier here, in spite of being alone, and if I can write you about success, it will counterbalance all the privations. And, I believe, that you too will enjoy me more from a distance, if you know that I am happy. We shall see each other quite often and write very often. . . . You want to know how I pass my days; then read: I get up shortly after seven o'clock, have breakfast, go for a walk usually until nine o'clock. . . ."

Mornings were devoted to Chief Justice Horace Gray who had engaged Louis as his law clerk. Brandeis had decided against the position with the magazine, feeling that it would be too demanding. It was a wise decision. For two years the salary that he re-

ceived from Judge Gray took care of his needs until
enough clients began to come to the offices of Warren & Brandeis.

"After lunch I go to our office, talk over our
business affairs with Warren, work there or in the
Law Library according as business requires, and
shortly after six o'clock I have dinner. The evenings
of last week I spent as follows. . . ." He then listed
his trips to the laundry, his sailboating, bathing, and
social visits.

His evenings were busy, and they grew busier.
Homesickness disappeared quickly as he joined the
Exchange Club, the Union Boat Club, the Dedham
Polo Club, the Boston Art Club, and an athletic
club.

"At present everything looks rosy here," Louis
told Charlie Nagel.

The two young barristers, Warren and Brandeis, didn't grow rich their first year, but they did
come through on the blue side of the ledger. Their
bank account showed a balance of twenty-four
hundred dollars, which meant twelve hundred
apiece. Brandeis had a way of winning cases, first
very small ones, then larger and larger.

Naturally his Harvard friends were among his
first clients, and they kept his interest alive in Harvard's affairs. When Professor Thayer told Brandeis
that the Law School wanted to endow a chair so that

Oliver Wendell Holmes could teach there, he was delighted. Ever since Sam Warren had introduced them
three years before, he and Mr. Holmes had grown
closer in their friendship. Brandeis sometimes spent
summer weekends at the shore with Mr. and Mrs.
Holmes. He knew at close range by then the talent of
the man who would one day become one of the great
liberal justices of the United States Supreme Court.
Holmes had just given a series of talks which he was
going to publish in a volume called *The Common Law*.
The book was to become a classic.

How large a fund must they create so that Harvard could have the benefit of Holmes's talent, Brandeis wanted to know. Professor Thayer told him that
ninety thousand dollars was needed. Brandeis had
no idea where the sum would come from until suddenly soon after, as he was crossing Boston Common, he chanced upon William Weld whom he had
once tutored at the Harvard Law School. Weld was
now a millionaire, young and idealistic, willing to
listen to Brandeis's appeal. "I will donate the entire
amount," Weld said a short while later, "if I may remain anonymous."

Leading people of Boston, who were becoming
Brandeis's clients and friends, stimulated his concern
for public affairs. They all seemed to be active in
public life somehow—in a political party, in big business, in social work. Brandeis grew interested in

their interests. And as a Boston voter he wanted to be as informed as possible on city and state politics.

He read the newspapers carefully, and some articles in the *Boston Globe* by John F. O'Sullivan soon caught his eye. O'Sullivan was writing about the national currency, and Brandeis had read and studied a great deal on currency and finance by then. While O'Sullivan's articles were extremely well written, his ideas were inflationary, Brandeis felt.

He was so disturbed by the influence O'Sullivan's articles might have that he could not rest until he met O'Sullivan and explained the error of his ways. The newspaperman was more than happy to meet Brandeis. The firm of Warren & Brandeis had already made a name for itself in Boston.

O'Sullivan was in his twenties, a tall square-faced man with a handlebar moustache. Brandeis found him forthright and enthusiastic.

"Actually I am a labor reporter," O'Sullivan told Brandeis. He listened amiably while the attorney discussed sound money policies. He listened and nodded, and sometimes agreed.

"I want you to come home with me and meet my wife," he said at last.

Brandeis accepted the invitation. Entering their home to teach, he stayed to learn—about a whole new side of Boston that he had never known, and about a new social movement: trade unions.

Mrs. O'Sullivan was Mary E. Kenney of Chicago.

"My wife is the first woman union organizer in America."

The first *what?* A *lady* organizing labor unions?

"I have just come from Chicago," Mary Kenney told him. "I had a conference there with Samuel Gompers."

Brandeis wanted to know about Samuel Gompers, and Jack and Mary O'Sullivan explained. Gompers had been apprenticed to a cigarmaker in London as a boy. When he immigrated to the United States, he found work in a Chicago cigar factory, joining the cigarmakers' union in 1864. Because he was a natural leader, he was soon holding one office in the union after another until he became president. By 1879 he was the most outstanding union leader and organizer in America.

Louis Brandeis would not be able to forget what the O'Sullivans taught him about unions and the necessity for them. They described terrible working conditions in the factories they had visited —too long hours for both men and women, and even for little children, pitiful wages, dangerous situations in the handling of machinery. Brandeis recalled the

recent rash of railroad strikes. Some of those men
had been striking for an increase to *a dollar and a half
a day*.

The O'Sullivans were stimulating, exciting, and
different. Brandeis learned from them that there was
a large Irish population in Boston and the region
around Boston—just as there was a large German
population in St. Louis. The Irish had come to
America as refugees, too—refugees from famine and
starvation. They had met unemployment, more starvation, discrimination. But because they had fighting
spirits, they were coming through it triumphant.

Boston was beginning to seem like his own. He
was really putting roots down here. Some day he
would know it as well as he did Louisville. As a lawyer he would be as much a part of the life of this
city as Uncle Lewis was at home.

When Harvard Law School offered him an assistant professorship in law, he did some careful
thinking, and finally declined. He did not want to
give up his legal practice. He liked the challenge of
new cases, the knotty problems that his clients
brought him. Trial work was especially stimulating.
Every case that he prepared and argued in court
added to his store of knowledge: estates, trusts, investments, manufacturing, transportation, unions.
And there was that deeper ambition—to be independent, to be free of having to work for money. He had

already made a good start in that direction, following the principle that a man must spend less than he earns to get ahead.

He was economical in everything he did. His office on Devonshire Street was furnished with the plainest of things. And he was economical with his time, too, making every minute of the day count for as much as possible. If someone had an appointment with him at three o'clock, Mr. Brandeis's secretary came out to the waiting room on the dot of three to say, "Mr. Brandeis will see you now."

He was economical with his clients' time as well. They particularly liked him for his brevity and directness. They could talk to him straight from the shoulder and get their advice back the same way. Nobody ever deceived him. If a client appeared with larceny in his heart, Louis Brandeis knew it and told the man so. Once he wrote in his memo book: "Some clients' prosecuting reminds one of the man who had no sheep and lost one."

In the courtroom he was quiet, gentle, and thorough. As he moved about during a trial, one hand in pocket, his logic was devastating, whether he was asking a witness question after question until he got the answer he wanted or addressing a jury.

Anyone who heard about him wanted to meet him. One evening when the young attorney Glendower Evans and his wife were calling on friends, they came to the front door just as Louis Brandeis and someone else were leaving. A brief introduction, and Brandeis was gone.

"Louis Brandeis is a man I have always wanted to know, and here he is leaving just as we arrive," said Evans.

"Why don't we ask him to dinner?" his wife, Elizabeth, suggested.

When Brandeis accepted her invitation, he picked up the thread of another important friendship. Evans he learned was a Philadelphia Quaker, and his wife had been Elizabeth Gardiner of Boston. Soon Brandeis began to feel like a member of their family, he was with them so much. Evans shared his love of boating. On Sundays the three of them often went on excursions in the coastwise steamer or canoeing on the Charles.

Life was good and growing better. As he worked in his office, argued a case in court, or strode along Beacon Street past the Common, Louis Brandeis experienced an increasing joy in pure living. He felt that Boston was changing his temperament. "Now I find myself as variable as the atmosphere—as unstable as a barometer," he said in one of his long letters to Charlie Nagel. "This morning I was boiling over with joy and in such a good humor that I could not keep quiet."

His letters weren't always long. More often they

were one or two sentences on a scrap of paper addressed to anyone he wanted to be in touch with at the moment. He and Alfred particularly liked to exchange one-sentence letters. Louis' might go on a piece of courtroom notepaper: "Do you remember that on this day in 1873 we were in Florence, Italy, and all the museums were closed." Alfred's notes often came to him scribbled on Western Union blanks. The two brothers wrote something to each other almost every day.

Their letters quite naturally contained more politics as the Presidential election year of 1884 rolled around. Brandeis had been losing patience with the Republican party. He thought, as a great many Republicans thought throughout the country, that too many reactionaries were in control. The real trend of the times was liberal and toward reform.

When the Republican party held its national convention in Chicago in June, it nominated James G. Blaine of Maine for the Presidency. Blaine was Speaker of the United States House of Representatives and a popular vote-getter. But there was ugly talk swirling around his head. He had even been investigated by Congress for using his position as Speaker to make profits on the side.

A whole section of the Republican party bolted as a result of his nomination and formed a third party, the Independent Republicans. They were soon being called "Mugwumps" in an effort to discredit them. But there were too many outstanding men among the Mugwumps for that plan to work: George William Curtis, one of the editors of *Harper's Magazine* and an old-time abolitionist was one; another was Carl Schurz, who was then Secretary of the Interior and respected by just about everybody. Still another was the rising young lawyer, Louis Dembitz Brandeis.

When the Democratic party nominated Governor Grover Cleveland of New York, the Mugwumps endorsed him.

Among members of the Democratic party Brandeis found more people willing to listen to ideas about the need for reform and more willing to accept the idea of change. The O'Sullivans were Democrats. They believed, as he was coming to believe, that life, times, conditions, must always keep changing. Dedicated men and women could make them change for the better.

That particular feeling grew in Louis Brandeis's heart. When he first came to Boston, he had joined only one or two social reform groups, because he was working so hard to build up the business of Warren & Brandeis. Now, after five years in Boston, he and Sam Warren were handling fewer and bigger cases for larger fees. His bank account was growing. He was beginning to enjoy a little freedom to serve on civic committees and even handle cases without charge, because he knew a favorable result would be good for Boston, or Massachusetts, or the United States—and everyone living there.

A change in the legal profession itself—in the way law was practiced—worked toward that end, too. In fact, it was a change that Brandeis himself pioneered—a new and expanded role for the lawyer. In the old days the lawyer had been an "advocate," someone called in after a person or company got into trouble. Gradually the lawyer became a "counselor" or adviser, someone who gave advice beforehand. Warren & Brandeis became counselors to several large corporations, giving advice not only on how to avoid illegal acts but in many other aspects of their businesses. Today this sort of law practice is widespread. Most companies and corporations have legal counsel to whom they pay an annual fee to advise them as they go along.

Louis Brandeis found his work deeply satisfying. But he never again made the mistake of overworking as he had at the Harvard Law School. Canoeing on the Charles River, horseback riding with Sam Warren, week-ending at the seashore with the Holmeses or Evanses kept him in trim. During the summer after Grover Cleveland's election he went off into the Canadian wilderness with friends for the whole month of August—walking, climbing, fishing, relaxing. Years later, when he looked back upon his life, he said, "I learned early that I could do twelve months' work in eleven, but not in twelve." His meaning was obvious: everyone must have a vacation every year. He almost always took the month of August.

And he had time for friends when they needed him. The sudden startling news of Glendower Evans's death took him immediately to their home and to the aid of Bessie Evans, to give whatever sympathy and compassion he could.

"Glen was only thirty years old!" she said, unable to realize what had happened.

Brandeis watched over her until she had recovered from the worst of her grief, then helped her decide how to find new happiness. She was well-to-do and did not have to be a slave to earning a living, he pointed out. With his careful guidance she found her way into welfare work, and soon she was a trustee of the state reform school at Benton, Massachusetts. Other useful positions followed.

He himself was becoming as much of a social reformer as he was a lawyer. Reform was on his mind most of the time, even when he wrote to his mother on her birthday:

> *I must send you another birthday greeting and tell you how much I love you; that with each day I learn to extol your love and your worth more—and that when I look back over*

my life, I can find nothing in your treatment of me that I would alter. You often said, dearest mother, that I find fault—but I always told you candidly that I felt and sought to change only that little which appeared to me to be possible of improvement. I believe, most beloved mother, that the improvement of the world, reform, can only arise when mothers like you are increased thousands of times and have more children.

He was beginning to realize how deep reform had to go in order to do any lasting good. Lobbyists spent huge sums of money—even bribed legislators —to get laws passed that would benefit their own interests. Reform here lay with the American voter, who must elect men to office who could not be bribed. Most of Brandeis's clients were top men in big corporations. Here, too, big business must be in the hands of excellent men, and there must be laws to regulate their conduct.

By 1889 when he was only thirty-two years old, Louis Brandeis ranked with the best of New England's legal men. Committees of the state legislature consulted him; he had already pled a case before the United States Supreme Court in Washington, D.C.; and had begun to appear in other states as a speaker before this bar association or that.

But suddenly that year there had to be a

change, when Sam Warren's father died. For this closest of friends, Brandeis had all the compassion and understanding that Sam needed. Warren was now head of his large family and all its holdings, suddenly involved with a multitude of important responsibilities. The two men realized what they must do: dissolve their partnership—after ten successful and happy years. Sam Warren would take over the management of the Warren family affairs and the paper mills. Their friendship would never end; they would occasionally work together; but they would see far less of one another in the future.

"I intend to keep the firm's name," Brandeis decided. "It will still be known as Warren & Brandeis."

Only a few weeks after he had moved his things out of the office, Sam wrote:

Dear Louis:
There is no need of wishing you a Happy New Year (tho I do) because a man who well and fearlessly faces every duty without a shirk is bound to have a Happy Year. Open all my letters, and send me those you think I want or ought to see.
Yours affectionately,
S.D.W.

Two months later a tragedy occurred in Louis Brandeis's own family.

His sister in St. Louis, Fanny Brandeis Nagel, had been in ill health for some time. As bulletins reached him about her, he became more and more worried. A few months earlier her small son, Alfred, had died of typhoid fever. The loss had plunged her into a depression that she was unable to shake off. When her second child, a little girl named Hildegarde, was born, Fanny developed childbirth fever. The doctors couldn't seem to help her. Then the most difficult news of all arrived: Fanny, only thirty-nine years old, had died on March 5, 1890.

Her grief-stricken brother set out at once for the West.

Chapter 6

A TRIBUNE OF
THE PUBLIC

*"The makers of our Constitution
undertook to secure conditions favorable to the pursuit of happiness. . . . They sought to protect
Americans in their beliefs, their
thoughts, their emotions, and their
sensations. They conferred, as
against the government, the right
to be let alone—the most compre-
hensive of rights and the right
most valued by civilized men."*

Fanny had been almost as close to him as Alfred. Oh, true enough, when he and Alfred were youngsters, they used to try to escape from their two sisters. But as they approached adult life, that had all changed. Fanny was the oldest, five years older than himself, someone with whom he had learned to talk and correspond about almost everything—books, people, even law. She had had a clear, fine mind and a sensitive, sympathetic personality.

When he reached Louisville, he found his parents crushed by the loss, grateful to have him back with them. Even though his own sorrow was as deep as theirs, his heart went out to his whole family—Uncle Lewis Dembitz; his sister Amy and her husband, Otto Wehle, and their children; Alfred and his wife, Jennie Taussig, and their little girls. He visited with them all, giving what comfort he could. His father's brother, Dr. Samuel Brandeis on Jefferson Street, would want to see him, and he called there, too.

Henry and Alice Goldmark were visiting Uncle Samuel. Louis remembered them from New York, the children of the famous and revered Dr. Joseph Goldmark—"None spoke like Dr. Goldmark." Henry was now an engineer, and Alice was no longer the little girl with whom Louis had played when he was visiting the Wehles and Goldmarks in New York. She had been six then; now she was twenty-four, slender and attractive, with straight dark hair brushed back from a low forehead into a roll at the nape of her neck, and large brown eyes. She was gracious and low-voiced, a pleasant, intelligent conversationalist; he was pleased to discover how well informed she was on national and world affairs. But she was rather shy, and he had to draw her out.

He learned that she had six sisters and three brothers. Helen, her oldest sister, had married Dr. Felix Adler, the religious philosopher who had founded the New York Society for Ethical Culture about fifteen years earlier.

They talked about Dr. Adler, who could not accept the ancient ceremonies and forms of the traditional Jewish religion. He believed that the emphasis ought to be on knowing the difference between right and wrong every day of your life. Louis' mother had said, "I believe that only goodness and truth and conduct that is humane and self-sacrificing towards those who need us can bring God nearer to us . . ." Apparently Dr. Adler had defined it.

If he ever came to New York, he would meet Dr. Adler, Alice promised. Louis would most certainly come to New York! He wanted to meet *her* again—soon—sooner than Dr. Adler.

She invited him to visit her any weekend that he could get down from Boston. He accepted, and as soon as he returned East, he began to make frequent trips to New York City, joining the warm family circle of the Goldmarks at their new address of 473 Park Avenue. Alice's mother was a Wehle—that made Louis and Alice second cousins. Often he found himself part of a large cordial group of both families. His courtship of Alice was most welcome to all of them.

Alice committed her joy to her personal diary. Sometimes her talks with Louis were "never to be forgotten." Another time she jotted down that he was "always thoughtful of others."

The Goldmarks had been spending their summer vacations in the Adirondacks for several years, and this year they urged the Brandeises to join them. It meant that Louis and Alice could have long happy days together, walking, boating—"we were on the water before breakfast. . . . His eyes are always upon me. We go down to the river and he tells me his story—we have found each other."

When he returned to his Boston office, several of his one- and two-sentence letters went out—at once: "I am engaged to Miss Alice Goldmark."

Sam Warren was delighted with the news, and wrote a long letter to Miss Goldmark right away. He was most anxious to know her, he said. He was only afraid that his true feelings about Louis might sound exaggerated and fulsome:

> *I know that his courage is high, his fidelity perfect, and his sense of honor delicate. For weap-*

*ons he has an acute and highly trained intellect,
and for motive power a high enthusiasm for the
right. I sincerely trust that you may be in Boston before long, and that Mrs. Warren and I
may have the pleasure of welcoming you to
Boston, and to that important part of our lives
which we have in common with Louis.*

Their wedding would take place on March 23,
1891, and that gave them plenty of time to find a
place to live and make all their plans. Since Louis'
practice was in Boston, that was where they would
live, and so the task of finding a house was his.

Suddenly he found himself involved in some-
thing he frankly did not enjoy at all—worrying
about property, a house, alterations, decorations.
Friends came to the rescue. Lorin Deland, a law-
school chum, encouraged him to buy a house at 114
Mount Vernon Street, next door to his own. Mount
Vernon Street starts at the State House on top of
Beacon Hill and runs down the hill westward toward the section called the Back Bay where the
Charles River widens into a kind of bay or lake. The
Warren house was at 67 Mount Vernon near the top
of the hill, and 114 was at the bottom of the descent,
just beyond Charles Street.

The house was modest, only three windows
wide, three stories and an attic high, of red brick.

One in a series of attached houses that hugged the sidewalk of uneven red brick, it was within easy walking distance of Boston Common and Brandeis's office in Devonshire Street, on the other side of the hill.

But it needed painting and papering, window shades, carpentry, plastering, and heaven only knew what else, and Louis was an *attorney*. Again the Delands—Lorin and Margaret—came to his rescue, first with advice, and finally Lorin took over the whole task of hiring workmen and supervising the renovations.

Long letters went back and forth between Louis and Alice in New York. The house he had chosen, he told her, "is not ideal, but all things considered it is the best that could be obtained." He wanted their furnishings to be plain and simple, and—he hoped she would agree—he wanted their lives to be plain and simple, too. A man must spend less than he earns to achieve freedom.

She agreed with her whole heart. In fact, she wasn't even interested in clothes the way some women are. Shopping for a trousseau was becoming a chore and nuisance.

"I don't know whether to be sorry or glad that clothes and the like seem such a nuisance to you," he replied, as though he were a little afraid he had overemphasized economy. "I believe in good clothes; it is only the unreasonable accumulation of them which is objectionable."

They were married at the bride's home in New York by Dr. Felix Adler, Alice's brother-in-law. Then, after a two-week honeymoon in the Berkshires, they returned to Mount Vernon Street. Alice understood well by then that she would have to assume full responsibility for running the household, because Louis was too lost in his work to think about it.

They agreed on how much they would spend each month to live, and it was enough to allow her two maids to take care of all the housework. They were usually Irish girls who lived in. Domestic help was plentiful and inexpensive then.

Even though Alice was a rather inhibited and shy person, she schooled herself to be a gracious hostess, always prepared when Louis brought home an unexpected guest for dinner. Shortly after they had settled in the Mount Vernon Street house, an old friend visited them. Alice had roast chicken, and quite naturally set the bird on its platter in front of her husband for carving. The moment he picked up the large knife and fork, it was apparent that he knew nothing of the procedure. He made a wreck of the food.

"Mrs. Brandeis," said the friend with a twinkle in his eye, "do you always serve minced chicken?"

From then on, for the rest of their married life, Alice did the carving.

Louis soon wrote to his sister Amy Wehle about his happy, efficient household. He was frankly grateful for its efficiency, because he needed to live undistracted with his law to do his best job.

He had full responsibility for the firm of Warren & Brandeis now, but he and Sam Warren still saw a great deal of each other. Sometimes out of their long conversations on knotty legal problems, a whole new idea or interpretation would develop that was of value to the entire legal profession.

One factor in particular bothered Sam Warren, and that was "yellow journalism." Because he and his wife were wealthy and active in the social set, there always seemed to be a society reporter snooping around them, attending their private gatherings by some devious means. The Warrens entertained a great deal, and all sorts of private details of their parties came out in the papers that specialized in that kind of journalism. Warren insisted that it was their right to be *let alone,* and Brandeis agreed with him. The more they discussed the problem of privacy the deeper their conviction grew that everyone was entitled to have his privacy respected. As a result they wrote an article, "The Right to Privacy." It was published in the *Harvard Law Review* a few weeks before Louis' marriage.

Their article pointed out that certain kinds of privacy were guaranteed by the Constitution, especially in Amendment IV, which states, "The right of the people to be secure in their persons, houses, papers, and effects, against unreasonable searches and seizures, shall not be violated. . . ." Warren and Brandeis had come to the conclusion that a person ought to have the right to keep his feelings and emotions private, too. Any kind of gossip-mongering, amateur or professional, was an invasion of privacy. The right to privacy included the right to be let alone. A person's letters and diaries could not be published without his consent. The essay was long and thorough, developing the idea that the law ought to protect the privacy of a person in every way, not just from invasions of his property.

Much of their thinking in "The Right to Privacy" was new and original—and history-making. One authority said that Brandeis and Warren had added a new chapter to American law.

In the early 1890's business law was Brandeis's most important area of work. He even gave a series of lectures on the subject on Saturday mornings at the Massachusetts Institute of Technology. Having to plan his lectures led him to subscribe to a newspaper-clipping service, so that he would be widely informed about what was going on in the world of business in all the big cities. Each day he opened the envelope full of clippings that came in the mail. The news formed a pattern. There were trends. Most disturbing was the unrest among factory workers.

The pattern became vivid when he read a shocking report of a strike of Carnegie-Illinois Steel workers in Homestead, Pennsylvania. The employees had joined a union: the Amalgamated Association of Iron and Steel Workers. When the company put through a wage cut, the union called the workers out on strike. The company then hired armed strike breakers. There had actually been a battle between paid soldiers known as Pinkerton strikebreakers, shooting from a barge in the river, and strikers who had barricaded themselves on the bank.

What had become of the right to protest?

The union movement was really national, Brandeis realized. He had been thinking in terms of local situations, conditions here and there, to which people like Jack and Mary O'Sullivan had called his attention. Louis Brandeis soon learned that Mary had been a witness to the Homestead strike, had actually seen workers killed with guns.

"It took the shock of that battle, where organized capital hired a private army to shoot at organized labor for resisting an arbitrary cut in wages, to turn my mind definitely toward a searching study of the relations of labor to industry," he said later.

All over America two things were happening.
First, industry was growing. New factories were
coming into existence to make goods that people demanded. Railroads were building new lines to carry
the goods, consuming more and more coal in their
locomotives. Factory workers, railroad employees,
miners, and all those in related jobs were caught in
the rush for profits, working under conditions that
were often dangerous and unhealthy for too long
hours and not enough pay. Second, there was the
movement to organize trade unions to represent the
workers and to speak for them. It had started in a
small way almost a hundred years before, but it had
been interrupted by the Civil War. After the war the
labor movement took on new energy because conditions were so pressing. By 1886 the American Federation of Labor had been organized in Ohio with
twenty-five member unions and Samuel Gompers as
its first president.

Brandeis believed that any man who adminis-
tered an industry or business should consider himself a professional. Business was a profession, a calling. The policies of businessmen affected the lives of
thousands of people. Men who made business their
calling ought to have a deep sense of responsibility
to the people they employed. They ought to realize
—or be made to realize—that democracy applies to
business as well as government. Workers ought to

have the right to discuss and vote on their working terms and conditions.

This was a turning point in Brandeis's career, and he knew it. From then on he worked in terms of the relationship between business and law—and politics, naturally. As a leading attorney, he decided to work to improve the ethics of the business world with better laws. Many large corporations were his clients by then, and their executives listened to his advice.

Because he was both courageous and brilliant, his fees as an attorney grew rapidly. By 1896, when he was only forty, Louis D. Brandeis was a millionaire—free—free to fight lobby groups that tried to bribe legislators, to fight the West End Railway when it tried to monopolize the city transportation system, to take up the cause of Boston's paupers.

But he never became too involved with causes to spend some time each morning with his two little girls before he set out for the office. An early and leisurely breakfast was his rule. Susan, born February 27, 1893, was three and beginning to understand what went on around her. She had deep brown eyes like her mother and straight black hair. Elizabeth, born April 25, 1896, was a brand-new baby. Her hair was coming in black, too, and her eyes were hazel.

Their mother was never robust, and so he added a children's nurse to the household. Sometimes Alice was overcome with nervous exhaustion and had to rest. He urged her not to come down for breakfast in the morning. One of the maids could serve him, and his daughters would entertain him.

Louis Brandeis was learning to handle some household matters, particularly their vacations and holidays. Now he must plan for four. Each spring he took them away from the dust and noise of the city to a cottage in Dedham, a Boston suburb. From there he commuted to work by train until the first of October. They all loved the seashore and always spent their August vacation somewhere on the New England coast—Block Island one summer, South Yarmouth another. August was still the twelfth month of the year in which he did no work. Then he belonged entirely to his family.

When they finally returned to Mount Vernon Street for the winter, they were all tanned and rested. Feeling fit himself, he would stride out in the morning to his office, ready for whatever lay ahead.

More and more the tasks ahead were public issues. The scrap over the West End Railway was one of them, filled with drama and dating back several years. In 1893 the West End had applied to the Massachusetts legislature for permission to lay tracks across Boston Common, that historic park! where soldiers had drilled in the American Revolution, where protest groups could always gather. To Brandeis the idea of running a railroad across its green lawns was outrageous.

That had been three years ago, the first time that Brandeis had really plunged into a public fight. His first logical step was research. He read and he studied about city railways, trolleys, and other kinds of public transportation, about the kinds of permits, or franchises, they needed to lay their tracks through a city and carry passengers. When his ideas were organized, he wrote to newspapers and civic groups, and did all he could to stir up public interest. His most effective effort was to address the Massachusetts legislature in person.

Those who heard him speak that day never forgot his quiet manner and his irresistible argument. He was better informed on the question of street franchises than anyone else in the chamber, and after he finished speaking, all of the legislators knew more about the question than they had before.

"Never before this morning," one of them told him, "has it been my good fortune to hear so logical, clear and convincing an argument on the very important question of street franchises as that made by you at the State House. I wish that your remarks could be printed and sent to every taxpayer in the city."

Most gratifying of all was to learn that the legislature had voted down the West End's application.

Now, three years later, transportation was becoming a hideous problem to Boston, especially in the business section, the oldest part of town with its narrow, crowded streets. There was a perpetual traffic jam. To make matters worse a trolley lumbered along Tremont Street, stopping and starting. The city of Boston began to build a subway under Tremont to eliminate the trolley, but the whole project bogged down in politics.

Shrewdly the officials of the West End Railway came to the rescue. *They* would run the subway, since transportation was their specialty, but they wanted a fifty-year lease.

Once again Brandeis mustered resistance of the press, civic groups, and leading citizens. He finally persuaded the state to reduce the lease to twenty years and require the railroad to reimburse the city for part of the cost of building the subway. In addition, the West End must remove the old trolley tracks from Tremont Street.

Many of Boston's most substantial citizens held stock in the West End Railway, and they felt very tight-lipped about having their profits curbed. What was wrong with giving the West End a fifty-year lease if it could put the subway into running order and ease the traffic problem? Because, Brandeis tried to make them see, the shorter lease could prevent railroad interests from acquiring a monopoly of all transportation in the city, thus charging whatever fares they pleased, and giving whatever kind of service they pleased. But many of the substantials refused to see and even snubbed Mr. and Mrs. Brandeis socially after the transit fight.

Social snubs were wasted on the Louis Brandeises. They had so many real and fine friends, and so many real things to do, that they never missed a few invitations to pointless parties. Alice had her home and children, and all the guests her husband brought to visit, sometimes for dinner, sometimes overnight. She was a delightful hostess, in spite of having to fight her shyness, and he liked company provided the people were interesting. He had a talent for making interesting people talk, and he was a good listener. Outside of her home, Alice Brandeis always had some community project. One of her long-term concerns was for adult education. She worked for years to persuade the board of education to establish evening classes for working people, and she finally achieved it.

One of their real and fine friends was the well-to-do social worker Mrs. Alice N. Lincoln. About the time of Brandeis's first fight with the West End, she was investigating the poorhouses of the Boston area, where conditions were deplorable. The paupers in them were among the most pitiful, depressed, ragged, and dirty human beings on earth. By 1894 Mrs. Lincoln was forcing public hearings and a full-scale investigation, and she asked Brandeis to act as her counsel.

"The public officials who are responsible for these poorhouses should be dismissed from office!" she said to him.

He had been following the whole thing in the papers.

"Punishing a few officials is no solution," he said. "The fault is with the system itself." These paupers were human beings, men, women and children, who had come to the poorhouses because they had nowhere else to turn. Charity itself was destroying their spirits. Under the present system they were being minded and cared for, whereas they ought to be taught to care for themselves. They needed a chance to win back their self-respect. Every pauper who was physically able should be given a job and made to work at it.

"This is another way in which law can be creative," was his view of it. "We need a new law providing for the rehabilitation of paupers."

At long last the city Board of Aldermen did conduct hearings, and Brandeis worked with Mrs. Lincoln while she testified at those hearings week after discouraging week. He himself visited the poorhouses and came away deeply shocked at the squalor and despair.

"Men are not bad, men are not degraded, because they desire to be so," he said. "They are degraded largely through circumstances, and it is the duty of every man and the main duty of those who are dealing with these unfortunates to help them up and let them feel in one way or another that there is some hope for them in life."

He and Mrs. Lincoln won through after nine long months. The aldermen did enact a law to overhaul all of Boston's public institutions. This was exactly the kind of thing he had wanted to be free to do! When Mrs. Lincoln handed him his fee of three thousand dollars, he donated it to several charities.

No matter what a person's walk in life, Louis Brandeis understood that he or she wanted to move up. If a person did not realize it, Brandeis was not above prodding him. If he was a pauper, then let there be a law giving him a chance to work and earn back his self-respect. If the person was an intelligent girl in her teens who thought she only wanted to be a stenographer in his firm, she must be encouraged to study and improve herself.

Miss Louise Malloch came to his office as a stenographer. She showed a flair for figures, especially investments, and Brandeis took the time to teach her the subject and encourage her to study.

Soon he had her assume responsibility for his own list of stocks and bonds. In a very few years she was his personal secretary, handling all of his investments. Miss Alice H. Grady, who would one day hold the post of Deputy Commissioner of Savings Bank Life Insurance in the state government, began with him in the same way.

He was always a resource of compassion, understanding, and love; yet he seemed very withdrawn, even rather strange, to many people who didn't know him well. He was often lost in his own thoughts, and this helped to create the impression. The correctness of his manner and dress helped, too. As he had once explained to Alice, he liked good clothes, correct to each occasion. Whether he was cantering along on horseback with Sam Warren, driving out to the country with his wife and daughters, dining with friends in the evening, his appointments were in order.

People who knew him well—like Sam Warren, Judge Oliver Wendell Holmes, then on the bench of the Massachusetts Supreme Court, and Professor James Thayer of the Harvard Law School— understood that his aloofness was not intentional. They knew the generosity that lay behind the manner. Judge Holmes wrote to ask, "My nephew, Edward T. Holmes, now 3rd year, wants to go into an office on leaving the Law School and I should be delighted if he could get with you. Will you let me know whether there is any chance for him?" He knew there would be a place for the lad in Brandeis's office. And the same thing happened when Professor Thayer spoke for his son Ezra. The firm of Warren & Brandeis had room for him, too.

Yet Brandeis never seemed more withdrawn than when he sat at his desk or moved through the corridor of his suite of offices. His entire staff felt in awe of him in some degree, especially young newcomers like Edward Holmes and Ezra Thayer.

His two chief assistants, William H. Dunbar and George R. Nutter, felt the most at ease with him. They were fellow lawyers who spoke the language of law and sat in conference with him while he worked out the arguments for a case. Like everyone else in the firm they were pushed forward into responsibility. Brandeis even let them go into court to represent clients when he might have gone himself. As long as they did the job well, why not? The more responsibility he let them have, the more freedom it gave him.

In a few years both men had a real measure of their own ability, and it made them ambitious. Yet as they saw it, every case they won went to the credit of the firm, Warren & Brandeis. They both wanted to build their own careers.

William Dunbar was from Roxbury, Massachusetts, six years younger than Brandeis, and a gradu-

ate of the Harvard Law School. He loved and respected his chief, knew he could trust Brandeis to be
fair, but he was deeply troubled within himself
because he had a serious handicap—deafness. He decided to set forth his whole situation in a long memorandum to Mr. Brandeis—his desire to make a reputation for himself, to work toward giving his own
name some individual value. But he admitted that
he knew his deafness was a factor, that allowances
were always being made for it: "I have endeavored
in thinking over the matter to give due weight to my
own disabilities and to balance the very real pleasures and advantages of the present arrangement
with the difficulties of a more individual career."

The absolute honesty of Dunbar's memo
touched Brandeis deeply. He respected Dunbar both
professionally and personally. His deafness was not
as serious a handicap as he seemed to feel.

"I would not want to lose either you or Mr.
Nutter from my staff," Brandeis told him. "Perhaps
you are receiving more personal recognition than either of you realizes."

As usual, Brandeis did not act hastily. He let
the question simmer in the back of his mind for several months. Sam Warren must be considered.

"Do you think you will ever return to the firm,
Sam?" he asked one day.

No, Warren replied. He had decided to remain
with the family mill interests.

Only after Warren's decision did Brandeis make any change. He took in both Dunbar and Nutter as his partners and changed the name of the firm to Brandeis, Dunbar & Nutter. He had meant what he said about not wanting to lose them, because he was becoming more prominent on the political scene, even in national politics. He needed such people in his office whom he could trust to handle his affairs when he was away.

Very shortly after the change in his firm, he was in Washington, D. C., testifying before the House Ways and Means Committee regarding a new tariff bill that Congress was considering. He returned to Boston in time for another franchise fight with another railroad.

The Boston Elevated Railway Company asked the Massachusetts legislature to amend its charter, permitting it to build and operate elevated or overhead trains, connecting the suburb of Roxbury on the south side of Boston with Charlestown on the north side of Boston, running under the city via the West End subway tracks. It would pay rent to the West End for the use of its tracks in the city. The project was vast, in many sections, including a bridge across the Charles River.

Brandeis discovered that the Massachusetts legislature had already granted the Boston Elevated permits to use many of the streets in Boston. The language of the permits, or franchises, was so tricky that they were practically perpetual and allowed the railroad to charge any fares it pleased.

The greatest danger, in his opinion, was the fact that the public did not realize what was happening. The Boston Elevated was well on the way to gaining a monopoly, or control, of all the transportation in and around Boston. The public would be the sufferers in the long run.

He wrote a long, careful letter to the editor of the *Boston Evening Transcript,* which the paper published, objecting point by point to granting one corporation control of so much.

An ugly rumor began to spread: "Who is paying Brandeis to buck the railroads?"

When Brandeis heard that, he wrote immediately to the president of the Boston Elevated: "I have been retained by no person, association or corporation, directly or indirectly in this matter, and I have opposed it solely because I believe that the bill, if passed, would result in great injustice to the people of Massachusetts."

But so few people really understood franchises, and the stockholders of the railroad were so influential, that the bill passed.

During the next three years, the railroad interests went on increasing their control over transportation, until other prominent men began to be alarmed. Edward A. Filene, of Filene's Department

Store, decided that it was time to organize public opinion. He and a group of men started the Public Franchise League, and men like Brandeis joined and helped.

Edward A. Filene and A. Lincoln Filene were the sons of William Filene who had begun in business with a small store years before. They had expanded it into a big establishment employing hundreds of men and women, and were the kind of businessmen whom Brandeis admired—they had a deep sense of social responsibility. They shared profits with their employees and invited employees to be on the board of directors of the company at a time when that kind of policy was almost unheard of. They even created an employees' board of arbitration to hear and settle their workers' grievances.

The Boston Elevated in 1901 asked the legislature to pass a bill giving the company control of just about every inch of transportation on the surface or under the ground in Boston and the area. Boston was growing so fast that it needed another subway under Washington Street. Once again the Boston Elevated wanted to build it, with a fifty-year franchise which would give it plenty of time to acquire control of anything else it needed.

The Public Franchise League was ready, and Louis Brandeis planned the fight against the bill: letters to editors, long memoranda to unions, merchants, and businessmen asking their support, and petitions to the members of the legislature. The campaign for and against the new franchise bill was top news for weeks—all over the country. Most cities in America were growing too fast, with all kinds of transportation problems. Their governments and businessmen watched the franchise battle in Boston with keen interest.

But in spite of all the league's efforts, the Massachusetts legislature passed the bill. Some of Brandeis's associates turned to him with that I-guess-we-are-licked look.

"Not at all! There is one more thing we can do."

What Brandeis meant was that he would do one more thing: Write to the governor of the state and ask him to veto the bill. "This bill will, if it becomes law, give to a private corporation a valuable monopoly for fifty years. It not only binds this generation, it ties the hands of the generation to come," his letter said.

Governor W. Murray Crane was a slender, energetic man and an effective administrator with a keen sense of what was best for Massachusetts. He did veto the bill, and both houses of the legislature upheld his veto. The message that he sent to them, along with his veto, contained many of Brandeis's arguments.

Louis Dembitz Brandeis had said long ago that

the only way to obtain good legislation and defeat bad is to arouse public opinion. He wrote a long, happy letter to Mr. Filene saying the same thing again.

Brandeis had a national reputation by now and was winning the respect and gratitude of people almost everywhere, as more and more of them realized that he was giving his time and talent free of charge to this sort of service.

"You are a true tribune of the public," Frank Taussig wrote to him from Harvard.

Chapter 7

A COUNTRY OF BALLOTS

*"There is a widespread belief . . .
that the true prosperity of our
past came not from big business,
but through the courage, the energy and the resourcefulness of
small men; that only by releasing
from corporate control the faculties
of the unknown many, only by re-
opening to them the opportunities
for leadership, can confidence in
our future be restored."*

His family thought so, too. Alice had realized for as many years as they had been married that he was a kind of knight righting wrongs, a knight of the law. But unlike the families of many dedicated men, she and her two daughters did not have to suffer from either privation or neglect.

A year earlier, in 1900, he had moved them to a larger home at 6 Otis Place. It was just off Mount Vernon Street, closer to the Charles River than their other house, on a short dead-end street. This house, too, was attached to others and made of red brick, with nine steps up to the front door and the entrance to the basement underneath the steps.

In those days the Charles River came up almost to the back of the house. When Louis Brandeis stood looking out at the view, he decided to ask the landlord's permission to put in a picture window, long before the idea became fashionable. From the new window they could see the glistening, wide Back Bay part of the Charles with its green banks and at night the blinking lights of Cambridge on the other side.

Much of the bay has since been filled in. Today another building blocks the view from Number Six, and traffic whizzes over an expressway between Otis Place and the narrowed river. But as long as the Brandeises lived there—nearly sixteen years—they enjoyed the water. In mild weather Louis Brandeis taught Alice and his daughters to paddle a canoe, and in the winter he took them to a place about a mile from the house where the river was narrow enough for safe skating. If the girls grew too tired to walk, he pulled them on their sled.

Wintertime indoors was problematical, when temperatures outside plunged down. The tall narrow house with its high-ceilinged rooms depended on a hot-air furnace, which never quite did the job. Elizabeth's room had no register and was terribly cold. Susan's room in the back of the house did have a register that gave out a little heat. Two gas heaters in the upstairs halls helped a little, and so did another heater in the bathroom.

Susan and Elizabeth were seven and four when they moved to Otis Place. Both had straight black hair. Elizabeth wore hers long, down her back; Susan's was short. Every morning they had breakfast with their father, clattering into the dining room in their high-buttoned shoes and starched white dresses. This was a time for conversation about history and current events, the time when Father made learning enjoyable. And it was a time for books. They took turns reading Thayer's *Short History of Venice,* or a history of Italy. Everyone's absolute favorite was *Kidnapped.* Father had told them the story when they were still too young to read it themselves. Father even gave them legal experience at an early age. They signed their first contract with him when they were eight and five, agreeing to polish his shoes six times a week, holidays excluded. For this each received five cents a week.

"Even though we were minors," Susan Brandeis said in later years, "we lived up to our contract for years during our summer vacations in Dedham."

In spite of owning a horse, kept at a nearby livery stable in Boston, with a buggy for fair weather and a sleigh for winter, Louis Brandeis always walked to work. Susan and Elizabeth walked part of the way with him, continuing their breakfast-table discussion. Sometimes they recited passages from Shakespeare as they walked along Brimmer Street to Beacon and across the Common as far as Tremont. There the girls turned back. Susan was already attending Miss Fisk's primary school and must be on time. Elizabeth would follow her there in another year.

When his daughters had gone, Louis Brandeis went on to his office in Devonshire Street.

On his desk the morning mail was ready for him. There was always a great deal of it, because the "tribune of the public," or "the people's attorney" as many were beginning to call him, usually had several issues and cases going at one time. And there were bound to be appeals to participate in more. "Able lawyers have . . . neglected the obligation to use their powers for the protection of the people," he once wrote. "We hear much of the 'corporation lawyer,' and far too little of the 'people's lawyer.'"

Family mail was delivered to the house: a letter from Alfred or Amy. Alfred was now handling most of the responsibility for the company of A. Brandeis & Son, because their father was nearly eighty.

One day there was upsetting news from Louisville: his mother was seriously ill, probably her final illness. Soon word came that she was gone. With Frederika Dembitz Brandeis's passing, the family realized that an era was coming to an end. Adolph Brandeis would live only four more years; Uncle Lewis Dembitz only six. Dr. Joseph Goldmark—none spoke like Dr. Goldmark!—had died in his early sixties. Soon there would be none to remind them of the Revolution of 1848. Their ties with Europe would cease, and only the American-born descendents would remain to carry on.

Louis Dembitz Brandeis carried on in the finest tradition of revolution—the peaceful revolution of gradual reform. During the first ten or twelve years of the twentieth century he accomplished so much in the way of reform that the very record is hard to believe. He defeated a great railroad monopoly, overthrew a monarchy in life insurance, launched the trend for better working hours for women, discovered the cause of Zionism, and became an adviser to the President of the United States.

His battle with railroad monopolies grew out of the times. The United States had been going through a railroad-building age for more than seventy-five years. The first railroads had been short lines, connecting seaports with the interior or with each other—the Baltimore and Ohio, for instance, and the Boston and Worcester. Then, as inventors improved railroads and made them safer, they grew longer and faster. The whole country was growing dependent upon them. They stretched southward and westward, replacing the stagecoach and the pony express, carrying people, freight, and mail: the Pennsylvania Railroad; the Union Pacific; the Missouri Pacific; the Southern Pacific; the Atchison, Topeka and Sante Fe; the New York, New Haven and Hartford. They spread out and prospered, and those who invested in railroad stocks made money. Speculators floated huge loans to build more railroads. Still they prospered—until 1893. That year the whole economy sagged—the way it had in 1873— and railroad stocks sagged with it. Lines that had borrowed too heavily went bankrupt when they could not find the funds to repay the loans. They were bought up by other lines.

Louis Brandeis had been deeply involved in

railroad financing as eastern counsel for the Wisconsin Central Railroad. The Northern Pacific Railroad gained control of the Wisconsin line. Then, when the Northern Pacific went bankrupt, the Wisconsin and whatever other lines it controlled went down with it. The line that Brandeis served had to be reorganized and put back on its feet. In the process of examining all its books and earnings and of working out a plan for reorganization, he gained priceless experience in this special kind of accounting.

This and other experiences advising corporations helped him to see right into the danger of monopolies. When two or more big companies competed with one another for business, that was good for trade; but when two or more combined to wipe out competition, so that they could charge whatever prices they pleased, that was combining to restrain trade. A monopoly was a way of giving too much power to too few people, sometimes to only one person, who gained control of a whole group of railroads or other companies by owning the stock of the companies.

A share of stock means exactly that: a share in the company. If a company issued a hundred thousand shares of stock and sold them, whoever bought any of the shares became a part-owner of the company. Each single share of stock gave a person one vote at stockholders' meeting. If a person bought ten thousand shares, he owned one tenth of the company. If he bought more than half, he controlled the company.

One wealthy man, or group of men, could buy up the stock of any companies they wished to control. Such monopolies could rule a whole industry, regulate prices, wages, working conditions, and the public had nothing to say about it. It was a kind of tyranny.

As monopolies, or trusts as they are sometimes called, grew bigger, there were many men in public office right up to the Presidency who understood the danger. Theodore Roosevelt—"Teddy"—was President of the United States from 1901 to 1909. He was a liberal Republican with a real concern for the public good and the courage to speak out. He led the opposition to trusts and monopolies. During his first term in office he succeeded in forcing a big railroad holding company, the Northern Securities Company, to dissolve. It had been created to hold the stock of other railroads, and the big financier behind it was J. Pierpont Morgan, whose aim was to control all the railroads in the northwestern United States. Morgan's attorneys fought the case up through the courts until the United States Supreme Court decided that the merger in the northwest violated the Sherman Anti-Trust Law, because it was a combination that restrained trade.

The publicity stirred up a lot of interest in the problem, and Roosevelt was reelected on a platform of "trust busting." He had no intention of destroying corporations, he promised, but they must show a sense of responsibility to the public.

Brandeis agreed with that. He considered bigness a curse when it was used to destroy fair competition. "Monopoly has a deadening effect, because it attempts to substitute a few minds for many minds." There were times when such combinations were needed to give efficient service, but the government must supervise them more carefully. Actually bigness led to inefficiency more often than not. Brandeis was convinced that there were limits to how much detail one individual at the head of a corporation could supervise. As he watched the large corporations grow larger, their services to the public did not necessarily improve; sometimes they went down hill, because the company had grown unwieldy.

The United States government was looking into the oil and tobacco industries as well. The Standard Oil Company, for instance, under John D. Rockefeller's direction, controlled 95 percent of all the oil refining in the United States.

Louis Brandeis was concerned about the railroads. He was grateful for the amount of public interest the Northern Securities case had stirred up when he took on the biggest fight of his professional

life so far—his fight to prevent a single interest from
monopolizing all of the transportation in New England.

The first big danger sign occurred in 1905. The
Boston & Maine Railroad applied to the Massachusetts legislature for permission to buy some connecting trolley lines in the state. But Massachusetts had
a law that no railroad corporation could hold the
stock of another corporation, and so the legislature
turned down the request of the B & M.

Then . . .

News began to circulate that the New Haven
was buying stock of the Boston & Maine.

Louis Brandeis lifted his head like a hunting
hound when he heard about it. The "New Haven"—
the New York, New Haven & Hartford Railroad—
was chartered in Connecticut. Its directors had a
way of ignoring the laws of Massachusetts. The company had already acquired about a third of the
street railway mileage in Massachusetts.

If the New Haven was buying stock of the B &
M, it could only mean that the directors of the New
Haven were planning to merge the two roads. This
would mean the company would control transporta-
tion in the whole northeastern part of New England.
Once again the money tycoon behind it all was J.
Pierpont Morgan. A couple of years earlier he had
used his controlling interest in the New Haven to

elect Charles S. Mellen as president of the line. Mellen was a seasoned railroad executive. He worked like a beaver to build up the New Haven, buying up every kind of competition—steamboats, trolley lines, suburban trains, and combining them all into one big system. He had been doing this all over New England.

Leading Massachusetts men, like Brandeis, Filene, and others, were profoundly worried. They knew better than anyone else how such a spreading monopoly could control the entire economy of the region. But none took it quite so seriously as Louis Brandeis, and none felt more personal concern than he.

When his secretary came in to his office to say that Mr. William B. Lawrence wanted to see him, Brandeis guessed in a second what it was about. Lawrence and his father, General Samuel C. Lawrence, were big stockholders in the B & M.

Brandeis asked Mr. Lawrence to sit down, and the visitor came right to the point. The remaining stockholders of the B & M wanted Brandeis to act as their attorney in the fight to prevent the New Haven from taking over.

Brandeis agreed and added, "I feel, however, that this being a matter of great public interest in which I am undertaking to influence the opinion of others, I do not want to accept any compensation for my services."

Lawrence was dumbfounded. Of course, they expected to pay him. Of course, they. . . . But the expression on Brandeis's face hardened, and so Lawrence kept his peace, said thank you, and left.

The people's attorney had been studying the New Haven situation for months. He had folders full of facts and figures. If the Morgan interests gained control of the B & M, they would have a monopoly on most of the transportation in New England and could charge any rates and fares they pleased for freight and passengers—and give any kind of service.

Brandeis detested greed. He could not understand men who spent their whole lives accumulating money for its own sake. Neither could he understand men who were as fixated on personal power as Morgan and Mellen. These men wanted to rule like absolute monarchs, but now that he was representing the stockholders of the B & M, he could lead, plan, and direct the fight against such greed and power. The Brandeis-Mellen fight went on for almost nine years.

When Louis Brandeis assumed his role as general-in-command of the struggle, he was already a prominent person. In fact, he was controversial, accumulating devoted friends and enemies at about the same rate of speed. His association with the B & M was front-page news. Public interest ran high, and that was all to the good.

His first move was to write a bill for the Massachusetts legislature to enact into law. The law would compel the New Haven to dispose of whatever B & M stock it already held.

There followed the usual public hearings in June 1907. Brandeis appeared to testify before the legislature; so did Mellen. They were both effective and well-informed speakers. Mellen had a lot of personal charm, and his "interests" were backing him up with favorable publicity, not to mention a powerful lobby.

After weeks of tension, debates, addresses, correspondence, and testimony, Louis Brandeis had to see the legislature vote down his bill. To make it even more discouraging, the legislature passed another bill in its place, permitting the New Haven and the B & M to merge. Many of the lawmakers genuinely believed that the merger would mean more efficient service.

Mellen was bursting with joy. He posed for cameras, granted interviews, made statements, had a long conversation with the governor of Massachusetts about the future of transportation. This would be good for the prosperity of New England, he declared.

But if Mellen thought he had won the war, he was mistaken. He had only won a battle. Brandeis also gave interviews to the press. "It is not a question merely of monopoly in railroads but monopoly of the whole transportation system," he told a reporter from the *Boston American*. "It would be like attempting to substitute a regulated monarchy for our republic. Human nature is such that monopolies, however well intentioned, and however well regulated, inevitably become, in course of time, oppressive, arbitrary, unprogressive, and inefficient."

A little earlier he had said something else: "Our country is, after all, not a country of dollars, but of ballots." He wanted to see those ballots distributed around among the many, not hoarded by the few, whether in politics or in business, whether ballots for a political candidate or shares of stock in a company.

A real source of comfort was the way his daughters followed the situation. They both had keen minds. Susan at fourteen could give a good statement of the issues in the New Haven merger case. Once during the recent hearings she had read in the paper that the New Haven had bought up the trolley line between Worcester and Providence. "Father," she had demanded, "where's the competition?"

Susan and Elizabeth were attending Miss Windsor's School in Beacon Street, within walking distance of Otis Place. When the school moved out to Longwood, they had to use the trolley. Susan planned to go to Bryn Mawr. Elizabeth declared she did not wish to be the "little sister" in college, and so she eventually went to Radcliffe.

They both treasured the time that he spent with them. He taught them much in an easy conversational way, yet he never preached or moralized. Often he taught by example. On Election Day he took them with him when he went to vote so that they would understand the procedure. Then after the polls closed, he took them downtown again to wait for the results, thrown on a big screen on the Boston Herald Building. When they were young, it meant being allowed to stay up long past bedtime; but as they grew older, they took it seriously because he did, realizing that some day women would be allowed to vote.

In her whole life Elizabeth could never remember seeing her father angry. Even though he was a supremely sensitive person, he never projected the upsets of his professional day on his family, least of all on his children. Instead he gathered them to him for comfort.

After his bill against the New Haven merger had been defeated in July 1907, he took his family to a rented cottage in South Yarmouth, Massachusetts, for August. South Yarmouth is on the southern side of Cape Cod in a deep harbor formed by the Bass River where it flows into Nantucket Sound. It is an old fisherman's town, founded in 1713 by the Quakers. The land around is flat farmland with some marshes and a nearby stretch of pine woods. Bass, bluefish, and clams abound.

The tidal creeks nearby were ideal for exploring, sometimes in their catboat, but more often in a canoe. The people's attorney and his two daughters would start out in the morning with sandwiches to be gone all day. He was an expert paddler who never took chances with his daughters' lives, using a long, slow untiring stroke against wind and tide. But he did give Susan and Elizabeth a taste of real excitement when he could.

One dangerous place was rocky Point Gammon. Here they could not paddle close to shore because of the submerged rocks and a swell. They usually dragged the canoe across the neck of land and launched it again on the other side. But one day Brandeis decided to circumnavigate the point. Starting out at five or six in the morning—he was always an early riser—he and the two girls settled into the canoe, eyes bright with excitement. He touched the paddle's blade to the water, and the canoe moved silently out into Bass River, then downriver and out into the sound. There was no wind; the water was calm. He paddled along the coast until they could see Gammon; then out to sea they glided, beyond the shoals.

A breeze started; a swell lifted the canoe. This was real danger! Skillfully Brandeis guided and maneuvered the canoe around the point, and at last they made it triumphantly into Lewis Bay. On the return trip they dragged the canoe overland and were home in time for lunch—glowing with a deep sense of achievement.

It was the kind of adventure that Susan and Elizabeth liked to relate to Captain Baker, a retired sea captain who had a small Cape Cod cottage near the highway. He had fixed up his barn as a kind of den with pictures of sailing ships on the walls and a huge chart of the seas. He had sailed several times around Cape Horn and never tired of telling them about his adventures, especially in storms. Captain Baker could understand better than many what a thrill they had felt in canoeing around Point Gammon.

The whole Brandeis family enjoyed South Yarmouth so much that they went there every summer for the next nine years.

On holiday or in Dedham Brandeis took his daughters on long walks in the fall and spring to explore a stretch of woods, to gather nuts or any other treasures they might happen upon. Sometimes they gathered too many items for their own pockets, and he always happened to have some cotton bags to accommodate them.

Back in Otis Place in the fall, the girls and their mother prepared their clothes for school, and he returned to his law practice, which included a great many cases as well as his continuing concern about the New Haven.

He had had a whole month to rest and reflect, and now his course was clear. He would make a complete study of the finances and bookkeeping of the New Haven Railroad and see for himself whether it was such a prosperous line.

He was appalled at what he found. The company was paying out more in dividends to its stockholders than it was actually earning and spending not nearly enough on upkeep and repair of its tracks and trains. If the New Haven and the B & M were to remain in business, they must reduce dividends and spend the money on services and repairs instead.

He published his findings in a pamphlet, *Financial Condition of the New York, New Haven & Hartford Railroad and of the Boston & Maine Railroad*. It went to the members of the Massachusetts legislature, to stockholders, newspapermen, and as many other influential citizens as possible—businessmen's groups, economic clubs, unions, lodges, lawyers' associations. He was invited to address many of their meetings in various New England cities, and he won some support wherever he spoke.

The day that the Department of Justice in Washington decided to look into the New Haven's affairs, the people's attorney felt profoundly encouraged. The United States District Attorney, Asa P. French, wanted facts and figures, which Brandeis could provide. As a result, the New Haven had to face a law suit under the Sherman Anti-trust Act, the same law that had brought an end to the rail merger in the northwest.

But Asa P. French was a member of President Theodore Roosevelt's administration. In November 1908 a new President, William Howard Taft, was elected. During the four years that Taft was in office, his Attorney General did follow through on cases against the Standard Oil Company and the American Tobacco Company. But the suit against the New Haven was allowed to drop.

The administration in Washington may have changed, but Louis Brandeis had not. He kept track of the activities of the New Haven system and its finances, making dire predictions. If they did not give better service to manufacturers, they would lose their freight business. Repairs too long neglected could lead to tragedy.

But the New Haven continued to bloom, taking on still more lines . . . until . . . Louis Brandeis's predictions began to come true. The New Haven's business began to fall off—less freight and fewer passengers. Its lines began to economize by laying off workers and being even more neglectful of repair. This led to worse service, fewer commuter trains, late deliveries, even wrecks in which people were killed or injured. New England manufacturers and businessmen were losing customers because they couldn't be sure of filling their orders. The New Haven's false front was collapsing.

In the 1912 election there was another change in the nation's government. The Republican party had split, putting two candidates in the field: Taft for reelection, Theodore Roosevelt as a Progressive. As a result Woodrow Wilson, the Democratic candidate, won the Presidency.

Louis Brandeis went to Washington to urge the new administration to start proceedings against the New Haven. This time he had behind him the support he considered most important—an aroused public opinion. Newspapers all over the country were reporting the deplorable state of the New Haven system. Voters were writing to their congressmen demanding action.

Finally, in the spring of 1913, the Interstate Commerce Commission began a formal investigation of the New Haven. The hearings were a national event. Telegraph wires clicked out the news across the country, and newspapers printed extra editions to bring word to their readers, the aroused public, in a "land of ballots not dollars." Reporters, photographers, attorneys carrying briefcases full of papers, crowded into the courtroom of the Federal Building in Boston.

The tall and slender Mr. Brandeis, now in his late fifties, hair graying at the temples, opened the hearings before the commissioners. Pince-nez in hand, he called as his first witness the member of the ICC who had examined the books of the New Haven. The man revealed a long list of shocking irregularities. The company exaggerated the value of its property, so that it would not appear in the red, which it was. For instance, two boats were listed as worth nine hundred thousand dollars when their market value was forty-four thousand dollars. The books showed an assortment of vague accounts such as "general expenses" and "special services."

The hearings went on, hour after hour, day after day, as newspapers reported their progress. A witness, cross-examination, another witness, cross-examination . . .

Brandeis had begun the hearings as the representative of the Boston Fruit and Produce Exchange, which had been seriously hurt by the bad freight service. But after two days that group decided to withdraw. The papers on the side of the

New Haven blared out that his client had repudiated him.

"It makes no difference," Brandeis explained. "I shall continue to conduct the investigation in the role of private citizen."

The rumor-mongering against Brandeis all during the hearings grew vicious. Who was paying him? What was there in it for him? Reporters who knew him published glowing accounts to counterattack his enemies.

"Why don't you reply to this evil talk?" one newsman asked him.

"A denial would only dignify their attack," he explained, "and I don't want to waste valuable time debating them that should be spent on this investigation."

The hearings had begun on April 22, 1913. Witnesses came to prove that the New Haven was an innocent victim of ruthless attackers, but the whole thing was going so badly for the line that by the first week of May the line's president, Charles S. Mellen, appeared in person to give evidence. Mellen was just as suave and able a man as Brandeis, and every bit as convincing a speaker.

"May I stand up?" Mr. Mellen asked the chairman.

Every gesture, every move that he made, was carefully dramatic. The spectators listened spellbound. Sometimes he walked up and down. Once he even leaned on the chairman's table for emphasis. There was just one flaw—his own ego. He could not resist the opportunity to boast of how he had built up a huge empire over the years. By gradually acquiring railroads, trolley lines, and steamship companies, the New Haven now had *absolute control* of rates in New England and as far west as Duluth, Chicago, and Milwaukee.

His own attorney tried to interrupt him, but he would not be interrupted. He cared more about having absolute control—and boasting about it—than he did about profits. He was ruler of a kingdom.

By the time the hearings ended, Mellen's career had ended with them. Stockholders were clamoring for his scalp, and so were most of the people in New England. Almost everyone in the region had been affected by his greed in some way—traders, shippers of freight, commuters, property owners. In July he faced his own failure and resigned.

That was not the end of the problem. Brandeis knew that the line could elect another president just like Mellen and continue in its old way. He stayed with the situation until all the shady finances of the railroad were exposed, and the whole complex forced to separate into its individual companies. The original New Haven Railroad would not pay a dividend on its stock for many years, not until it got its own budget balanced and its trains and tracks back into something like a state of efficiency. The Department of Justice finally made the New Haven give up the Boston & Maine, too, as well as its trolley and steamship lines. The company complied, and that was the end of that short-sighted monopoly.

"Size is not a crime," Louis Brandeis wrote later, "but size may become such a danger in its results to the community that the community may have to set limits. . . . Concentration of power has been shown to be dangerous in a democracy."

In the years ahead new laws would be enacted to prevent such situations from arising again.

"The great achievement of the English-speaking people is the attainment of liberty through law," was Louis Brandeis's conclusion.

Chapter 8

LIBERTY
THROUGH LAW

*"To stay experimentation in things
social and economic is a grave responsibility . . . . It is one of the
happy incidents of the federal system that a single courageous state
may, if its citizens choose, serve as
a laboratory; and try novel social
and economic experiments without
risk to the rest of the country."*

Liberty through law! Louis Brandeis believed in that idea as deeply as the statesmen who had written the Constitution of the United States and created our government more than a century earlier. He devoted his life to making it a reality for more and more people.

During the early years of his battle with the New Haven, he accomplished a victory in another field of business that he himself felt was one of the most important contributions he ever made. It was one that would benefit every family in America, and the lower the family's income the greater the benefit. The dull, little-understood subject of life insurance became for him a great cause, another area in which he could free people from a terrible burden by creating a better law to protect them.

There had been something of a scandal involving one company, the Equitable Life Assurance Society in New York, over the way one of its officers was handling the company's money. Brandeis read about it in the papers. The voters in New York State demanded an investigation, and the legislature appointed a special committee for the purpose.

The Equitable was one of the giants in the life insurance field. Many of its policyholders were Boston businessmen, who now became alarmed. If there were shady practices in one insurance company, what about the others? And so they organized the

New England Policy-Holders Protective Committee.

Early in 1905—the same year that Brandeis began his battle with the New Haven—the members of the Protective Committee called upon him at his offices and asked him to be their counsel. They wanted him to make a complete investigation of conditions in the life insurance field.

He agreed, and then said something that always startled clients: "Yes, you can retain me, but you must pay me nothing. I must be free to act according to my conscience."

One of them opened his mouth to protest and then shut it again.

"This matter is not private but public," Brandeis went on, "and I don't care to be paid for public service. Accept my services gratis or leave them."

They knew they needed him, that no one else would handle the job as well, and so they agreed to the strange arrangement.

Brandeis researched the whole life insurance field, checked the accounts and methods of the leading companies, and assembled some appalling truths. In October he spoke to the members of the Commercial Club of Boston and gave them his findings. There were about ninety life insurance companies in the country, he told them, with insurance policies on ten million people. Of the ninety, the three biggest were the Equitable, the Mutual Life of New York, and the New York Life. They were all Wall Street companies and had close connections with giants handling other kinds of insurance, such as the Metropolitan Life and the Prudential.

These companies were so wealthy and their combined assets so huge—more than $2,500,000,000— that they were an "economic menace." Out of every dollar paid in by policyholders as premiums on their policies, forty cents went to the company for huge executive salaries, elegant quarters, commissions to insurance salesmen, and dividends to stockholders. Worse still, if a working man lost his job and could not keep up his premiums, his policy lapsed, that is, he lost all or most of the payments he had already made.

Of course, Brandeis had remedies to suggest. These financial monsters ought not to be allowed to grow so large. The law ought to limit their size. Commissions and executive salaries ought to be reduced. The state should supervise their dealings, and they ought not to be allowed to lapse policies.

"Life insurance is essential," he reminded the men in the audience, and they had to agree. The lower a man's salary the less savings he was likely to have and the more important it was to him to protect his family with life insurance. "If our people cannot have life insurance at a proper cost and through fair, private agencies, then the resort is state insurance."

He himself understood something else now, better than he had ever understood it before: the real monopoly behind all other monopolies was money itself. Rockefeller millions had created the first oil trust; Morgan money had made it possible for him to gain control of New England transportation. And here money had done it again.

About the same time that Louis Brandeis brought out his findings, the committee for the New York state legislature brought out theirs. After long public hearings, their report revealed the same set of facts. The condition of life insurance was appalling.

It was worst in industry. There an agent came around every payday to collect a weekly payment from the factory workers. Sometimes the payment seemed small—fifty cents a week, perhaps—but at the end of a year the amount was outrageously high for the amount of protection a policyholder received.

The New York state legislature passed some laws to reform the worst of the situation there, but Brandeis did not consider them sufficient. Perhaps Massachusetts could do better.

Massachusetts was always out in front with progressive ideas, especially laws that protected the rights of the individual. It had been the first state in 1888 to adopt the secret ballot, so that each voter could truly vote according to his conscience without fear. Its labor laws were then the best in the country. Why should Massachusetts not be ready to improve its insurance laws?

Louis Brandeis never depended on "the other fellow." If Massachusetts needed a new law, it was up to him to write it.

Working with him at that time was Miss Alice H. Grady, who had been his personal secretary for nearly twelve years. He discussed the problem with her many times. Back in 1874 the first insurance commissioner of Massachusetts, Elizur Wright, had suggested that savings banks could handle life insurance, but nothing had been done about it. Now Louis Brandeis wondered whether that might possibly be the answer.

It meant still more research, but what of that? This time he did something that he almost never did. He took work home each evening—big thick reports of the Commissioner of Banks and the Commissioner of Insurance, which Miss Grady packed into a suitcase for him.

Late afternoons and evenings were usually kept for his family and for recreation—he often went horseback riding after work. But for a while he spent those hours at the dining-room table, opened out to its full length since no desk would have been big enough. Alice watched in amazement, and sometimes Elizabeth Evans dropped in to be just as amazed by the sight. He focused on the pages as though he were spellbound. This subject of life insurance had taken hold of him. It affected *so many*, almost everyone. A whole new method of handling it must be found; *he* must find it.

By the late spring of 1906 he had.

"Miss Grady," he said one morning, "we have found the answer. The savings bank can be adapted to the writing of life insurance."

He drew up a bill, the text of a future law, permitting savings banks in Massachusetts to sell life insurance. It would mean a tremendous saving to the policyholder—no agents' fees, no separate offices, no stockholders clamoring for dividends. A bank would probably have to add one or two staff members, and that would be about the only extra expense involved.

Brandeis did not leave the enactment of the bill to chance. He had known for years the importance of aroused public opinion. Skillfully and thoroughly he settled to the task of winning public support for the proposed law, sending out letters and news releases to every leading citizen, civic group, and newspaper. He wrote an article called "Wage-Earners' Life Insurance," which appeared in the September 1906 issue of *Collier's Weekly*. Norman Hapgood was the editor there. He was so impressed that he went out of his way to meet Brandeis. Their enduring friendship began at that point.

When the Massachusetts legislature convened for its winter session of 1906–1907, every member had before him a copy of the magazine article and a stack of mail from his constituents urging him to vote for the Savings Bank Insurance Law. Of course, Brandeis had stirred up opposition with his campaign, especially among those in the life insurance field whose profits would be reduced if this bill went through. But the measure passed, and was signed into law by the governor in June 1907.

Happy, gratified, tired, Louis Brandeis could walk across the Common to his home in the Back Bay, sink into an easy chair, take off his glasses, and rest his eyes. His own joy was reflected in the faces of his wife and two girls. He did not have to explain to *them* that as Massachusetts was the only state to have such a bill, he would go on for the rest of his life encouraging other states to adopt the same kind of law. The commercial insurance companies would be forced to give up their old practices and treat policyholders fairly in order to compete with the savings banks. They would have to lower premiums and stop lapsing policies so ruthlessly in state after state.

In this same month he would testify before the Massachusetts legislature against the New Haven merger and have to face his defeat when it voted down his bill on that subject. But this victory in the life insurance field was to him far more important.

Soon he and Alice, Susan and Elizabeth, would go down to South Yarmouth for canoeing, sailing, and Captain Baker's yarn-spinning.

The year 1907 seemed to be one of great causes for the people's attorney. One day in the fall he came home to learn from the maid that two ladies were waiting for him in the library. He hurried in and found Alice's sister, Josephine Goldmark, and a distinguished friend of hers, Florence Kelley.

He knew Mrs. Kelley. She had dedicated most of her adult life to social reform. From a well-to-do Philadelphia family, her father had been a member of the United States Congress for something like thirty years. He had taken her to a steel plant and then a glass factory when she was twelve, intending to impress her with America's industrial progress. Instead she had seen little boys working as helpers in the blaring heat of the steel furnaces and glass blowers' fires. She never forgot it. One of the many social evils she fought all her life was child labor. She was nearly fifty now and secretary of the National Consumers' League.

Louis Brandeis clasped her hand warmly and begged both ladies to be seated.

"Tell me about it," said he in his gentle, concerned way.

They did, and it was this. The state of Oregon

had a law which said that women in factories and laundries could work no more than ten hours a day. Curt Muller, who owned a laundry, had been arrested for breaking the law by working his women employees overtime. Tried and convicted, he had appealed to the state supreme court which upheld his conviction. The law was valid. Now Muller's lawyers were stubbornly taking his case to the United States Supreme Court.

Mrs. Kelley was a rather turbulent person, growing excited as she talked. "You see what can happen," she pointed out. "If the United States Supreme Court throws out the law, it could mean that labor laws in other states which have them could be lost."

Groups like the Consumers' League and labor unions had been working for years to get laws passed limiting working hours, setting minimum wages, and requiring safe working conditions, especially around big machinery. But there were still too few states having laws that protected the health and rights of workers. The idea was new and considered radical. Many lawyers and legislators believed that such laws violated the rights of the property owner or employer.

"There is still so much to be done along these lines, Louis," said Josephine Goldmark. "We mustn't lose what ground we have gained so far."

He knew. He had been close to the labor movement and its achievements ever since his early days in Boston.

"Will you defend the Oregon labor law before the United States Supreme Court, Mr. Brandeis, as counsel for the National Consumers' League?" Mrs. Kelley asked.

He was standing by the window, looking down at the peaceful, glistening Charles River. The two women kept silent as he thought. At last he nodded and turned to them. "Yes, I will take part in the defense."

Florence Kelley and Josephine Goldmark looked at each other with tear-blurred eyes. They had been friends a long time, working together in the Consumers' League and other groups fighting child labor. Now they worked with Louis Brandeis to help him assemble the information he needed to argue the case.

"I must have records of all the testimony given at legislative hearings. Get me the reports of factory inspectors and social workers. Let me have medical data from doctors about the effect of overwork on a woman's health, and data on how fatigue cuts down efficiency. Trade unions should be able to help you here. Above all else, be sure the information is absolutely accurate, so that I can quote it in court."

What kind of legal brief was this! They had expected him to send his clerks into a law library to look up other cases; for a brief—the statement of the client's case and all the arguments to support it—was usually based on previous cases which had been argued and decided on similar questions. He was not going to dig into the past for legal precedent. He was going to use the facts of human life today.

And he must have it all in two weeks. Two weeks? Yes. The women felt as though they had better run to the railroad station.

He had given them an impossible task, but they did it anyway. Out of all the material they gathered, and out of his own abundant knowledge, he wrote the famous "Brandeis Brief." When the United States Supreme Court heard the case of *Muller v. Oregon,* it heard a new kind of legal argument, related not to the past, not to precedent, but to life in our times.

Two lawyers for Mr. Muller and two for the state of Oregon together with the Attorney General for Oregon appeared before the nine black-robed justices to present their arguments. According to custom, the chief counsel for the plaintiff, Mr. Muller, presented his arguments first. The presentation was excellent. He spoke about personal liberty. If a person *wanted* to work more than ten hours a day, the law had no right to interfere. He cited previous court decisions to support his argument.

Brandeis listened intently. Then he rose to present his history-making brief. "Slowly, deliberately, without seeming to refer to a note, he built up his case from the particular to the general, describing conditions authoritatively reported, turning the pages of history, country by country, state by state, weaving in with artistic skill the human facts . . ." was how Miss Goldmark described it.

He spoke not of *legal* rights but of *human* rights. He urged the learned men on the bench to think in terms of America today and tomorrow. The country was growing more and more industrial. Factories were springing up, and they needed supervision and regulation. Conditions for workers must be made healthy and safe by law. That was why twenty states in the Union had already passed laws to protect the health and safety of women in factories and limit the number of hours they could work:

> *Fatigue which follows long hours of labor becomes chronic and results in general deterioration of health . . . weakness and anaemia undermine the whole system. . . . The universal testimony of manufacturing countries tends to prove that the regulation of the working day acts favorably upon output. With long hours, output declines; with short hours it rises.*

In using this new and unusual kind of social argument before the Supreme Court, Brandeis succeeded in persuading the justices to think in terms of "human justice." He made them realize that American society was taking urgent steps to meet new crises and that the court should let this important work go forward. And he won the case. The decision of the court was unanimous.

Immediately afterward, the "Brandeis Brief" was printed and its valuable data widely used by other lawyers, social workers, legislators, and unions. Oregon created an Industrial Welfare Commission which set standards for wages, hours, safety, and health in the state. When another case came up through the courts to challenge the right of the new commission to set minimum wages for women, Louis D. Brandeis represented the commission before the United States Supreme Court.

One of the judges of a lower court wrote to a friend after the case, "I have just heard Mr. Brandeis make one of the greatest arguments I have ever listened to. . . . He not only *reached* the Court, he *dwarfed the Court,* because it was clear that here stood a man who knew infinitely more, and who cared infinitely more, for the vital daily rights of the people than the men who sat there sworn to protect them."

Rights of people, needs of people. . . . In another year Louis Dembitz Brandeis was to look into the deepest human need of a people that he would behold in his entire life.

In July 1910 he and his family and Alice's sister, Pauline Goldmark, were on a vacation trip in New Hampshire, when he received an urgent message from A. Lincoln Filene, owner with his brother of the Boston department store. Some of the garment workers in New York City had gone on strike, and the strike was spreading. It was gradually paralyzing retail trade, because stores could no longer purchase garments to stock their shelves. Filene was as progressive as his brother in encouraging unions, fair pay, and decent working hours. Feeling that the workers were justified in their strike, he intended to go to New York himself and look into the situation. He wanted Brandeis to go with him.

Brandeis declined. He knew the strike was going on. It had started on the third of July, when ten thousand cloakmakers crowded into Madison Square Garden to vote on the strike. Cutters, pressers, sewing-machine operators, buttonhole makers, were all eking out a living making cloaks, skirts, and suits in the most sordid working conditions of any industry in America. They worked in sweatshops in tenements for small operators who competed with one another on cutthroat terms. For several years the Cloak and Suit Makers' Union had been organizing the workers and growing strong enough to represent them. When the first ten thousand walked out, others followed. More workers crowded into the union rooms on Tenth Street to join the union, so that they, too, could demand a living wage, shorter hours, something better than firetraps to work in. By now sixty thousand were on strike.

But Louis Brandeis shook his head. This was not his cause. The union was demanding a closed shop, which meant that a worker would be forced to join the union in order to work. That was too undemocratic for his taste. The American people, he felt, would not accept unionism if it involved the closed shop. "They will not consent to the exchange of the tyranny of the employer for the tyranny of the employee."

But the strike went on, growing more violent as people already starving grew desperate and rioted in the streets. Filene pleaded with both sides—the Manufacturers' Protective Association and the union —to meet in a conference. How could they ever settle anything, if they weren't even willing to discuss their differences? But the situation was deadlocked. The union insisted on a closed shop. The manufacturers would not recognize the authority of the union.

Knowing Brandeis's talent for handling people, Filene begged him to come to New York and try to bring the two sides together in conference. Sending his family on to South Yarmouth, Brandeis came. But, of course, he came on certain terms: the union must give up the idea of a closed shop during these conferences, and the manufacturers must listen to the grievances of the workers. Both sides agreed to meet—and on his terms.

When he reached the Lower East Side of New York, he discovered a world he had never known before. Crowded, unhealthy, it was as evil as any ghetto in Europe. People lived many to a room, in neglected, unsafe tenements, and they worked in the same kind of buildings. Their stores were pushcarts, standing along the curbs of narrow, crooked streets where the garbage collector and street cleaner never bothered to come. Poverty, utter poverty, and these people who worked such long hours for not enough wages were willing to go unemployed for weeks, actually starving, to obtain the right to work no earlier than eight in the morning until no later than eight-thirty at night, to arbitrate their wages, and demand the simplest of sanitary conveniences. This was certainly an uprising of utter desperation.

Most of them were Jewish immigrants from eastern Europe, refugees from unbearable conditions there. Here, in America, they were no better off. They were Brandeis's own people, these thousands of unemployed milling through the streets, shouting and shoving, growing more violent with each passing day, and he was part of them. He was glad he had come; he must find them a way.

The conference opened in a private room in the Metropolitan Life building. Ten representatives of the employers sat on one side of a long table, ten for the union on the other. Each side had brought an attorney to speak for it; each side was hopeful. The manufacturers knew they could trust the chairman, Louis Brandeis, to be fair. The workers knew he had won the Oregon case in the United States Supreme Court.

"Gentlemen," Chairman Brandeis began, "we have come together in a matter which we must all recognize is a very serious and an important business—not only to settle this strike, but to create a relation which will prevent similar strikes in the future."

The discussions dragged on for three days. The union continued to demand the closed shop; the manufacturers would have no part of it. The conference became hopelessly deadlocked. Louis Brandeis warned that both sides must realize that they would have to give in on some of their demands if anything was ever to be accomplished. Since he was everybody's only real hope, both sides pleaded with him to stay.

He began to clarify his own thinking. In spite of the terrible anguish of the ghetto and the tensions of that deadlocked meeting, his orderly mind was able to design a new possibility. In a few days he found that he was presiding over a more reasonable group of men, each side ready to listen to the other.

Workers' grievances included low wages, unreasonable night work, working in filthy tenement buildings, disregard of holidays and Sundays, irregular payment of wages, blacklisting of active union men. All these could be considered if they would give up their demand for a closed shop, that is, a shop in which only union men would be permitted to work. Here was the impasse, and to get over it, Louis Brandeis proposed a brand-new idea in labor relations: the preferential shop.

In a preferential shop the employer would be required to hire union members first, but if no union men and women were available for a particular job, then he could hire nonunion workers. In Brandeis's own words, "The preferential union shop is this: It is a shop in which union standards and conditions prevail, and in which the employer agrees, other things being equal, that he will employ union men—that he will give the union man a preference over a non-union man."

The idea was so completely new that both sides needed time to think about it, but at last they did accept it. Filene called it "brilliant." The discussions went on for almost the entire month of August, taking up grievances one by one. At last on September 2, 1910, the strike was settled; most of the workers' demands for better wages and hours and healthier working conditions had been met.

And Brandeis had guided both sides into accepting yet another provision: a "Protocol of Peace." This was an agreement under which there would be a board of arbitration to hear future problems and conflicts. It would mean orderly collective bargaining between capital and labor, between employer and employee, working out their grievances peaceably instead of starving through long strikes. The protocol kept peace in the industry for more than a year. It set a model for constitutional government in labor relations: an agreement between workers and employers as the basis for communication between the shop and the industry, with arrangements for handling grievances when either side thought the agreement was being violated.

When the settlement and the Peace Protocol were announced, the mobs in the streets of the Lower East Side turned into cheering, celebrating crowds. They had been idle for nine weeks. Now they could return to work for higher wages and better conditions. Most important of all, they could expect still more improvement in the future.

Looking so deeply into their misery, Louis Brandeis had caught a vision of something else: Zionism, the dream of Jews everywhere that they would one day have a country of their own. These poverty-stricken immigrants in the New York City ghetto needed the Palestine dream. They needed the hope of liberty through law—their own law, in their own land.

Chapter 9
ZIONISM

"Let no American imagine that Zionism is inconsistent with Patriotism. Multiple loyalties are objectionable only if they are inconsistent. . . . Every American Jew who aids in advancing the Jewish settlement in Palestine, though he feels that neither he nor his descendants will ever live there, will likewise be a better man and a better American for doing so."

Shortly after Attorney Brandeis returned to Massachusetts, a reporter from the *Jewish Advocate* of Boston interviewed him and asked how he felt about Zionism. Brandeis made his first public statement on the subject:

> *I have a great deal of sympathy for the movement and am deeply interested in the outcome of the propaganda. These so-called dreamers are entitled to the respect and appreciation of the entire Jewish people. . . . I believe that the Jews can be just as much of a priest people today as they ever were in the prophetic days.*

After his deep emotional experience on the Lower East Side, Louis Brandeis felt a need to learn more about the religion and history of his own people. Most of it was new to him, since his parents had never belonged to any synagogue or given him and his brother and sisters any training in a formal religion. But the garment workers' strike had made him much more aware of his Jewish background.

There had been a spark of interest in his mind for years regarding Zionism. As far back as 1897 when the first Zionist Congress met in Basel, Switzerland, he had read news items about it with sympathy.

"Now *there* is something to which I could give myself," he had said to Alice at the time.

Theodor Herzl, a journalist born in Hungary, had been responsible for bringing the first congress together, and he is known today as the founder of modern Zionism. Seeing the sufferings of the Jews in Eastern Europe—in such countries as Hungary and Russia—people of the same background as those Brandeis had seen in the Lower East Side—made Herzl decide to devote his life to their liberation. A year before the first congress he published his book *The Jewish State*. He wanted the ancient Jewish state restored in Palestine as a place of refuge and dignity for Jews, and it was this idea that the delegates discussed at Basel. There were many different viewpoints at that conference. Some believed that the idea of a Jewish national homeland was symbolic, that it existed anywhere that Jews could find security and freedom. Others believed that a specific country should be created in Palestine. The big achievement of the first congress was that Jewish leaders began to establish Zionist organizations all over the world.

The idea of a Jewish nation in Palestine was older than the Bible. Palestine, called Canaan in the Old Testament, was approximately the region bounded by the Mediterranean Sea on one side and the Jordan River on the other and touching Egypt on the southwest. In Biblical times, under kings Saul, David, and Solomon, Palestine had been a Jewish kingdom. But later it was conquered by Alexander the Great, then by the Romans. After that the Mohammedans ruled it, until the ninth century when Egypt took over. Later it became part of the Turkish empire, which lasted until World War I. During those centuries religious history had been happening in Palestine, and it became the holy land of three great faiths: Judaism, Christianity, and Mohammedanism.

To Jews all over the world who had no country of their own, who lived in other people's lands and under other people's laws—some liberal, some cruel —Palestine was the one place on earth of which they could dream as becoming their homeland some day. They could not all fit into that little space; but they did not all need to or want to. Many did not believe in Zionism and thought that Jews should assimilate wherever they were—just about as the Brandeises had done in Kentucky and Boston. Some believed that the Jewish state need not be in Palestine, that Jews ought to create their nation where there was more space, in South America, for example.

The spirit of Zionism was reform, which seemed to fit in so well with a general spirit of reform that was growing in America. Louis Brandeis was very deeply a part of that reform movement—the reform of working conditions, care of children, business practices. In politics the reformers were "progressives," and as the Presidential year of 1912 approached, progressive candidates grew more prominent. Progressive Republicans began to campaign for Robert La Follette of Wisconsin; the Socialist Party nominated Eugene V. Debs of Indiana. Many Democrats were talking of Governor Woodrow Wilson of New Jersey as a possible candidate for President even though he was far from the top of the party's list. All three men were liberals.

Brandeis was a Republican at heart, but he wanted the Republican party to be liberal and forward-looking, and to him La Follette was the man to make that possible. He and Senator La Follette had met in Washington, D. C., several years back, and they at once became friends. "I like Mr. Brandeis the best of any one we know," the senator once said to his wife. As far as Brandeis was concerned, Bob La Follette—short but powerful of build, dubbed "Fighting Bob" by newsmen—had the executive ability for the Presidency. And he had as well the courage, honesty, and—most important—a concern for the public interest. He had been governor of Wisconsin for six years, fighting the political machines and the politicians to give the state tax reforms, better election laws, and other improvements. Brandeis became his most outstanding supporter in Massachusetts. But in spite of all he and workers in other states could do, the Republican Convention in June 1912 renominated William Howard Taft.

To Brandeis, Taft was utterly unacceptable, a lazy administrator, lacking both concern and imagination. Many Republicans were frankly disgusted by the choice. Theodore Roosevelt was so disgusted that he stormed out of the Republican Convention and started a third party, the Bull Moose, with himself as candidate for the Presidency. Brandeis was not as certain of Teddy Roosevelt's concern for the public interest as he had been of La Follette's, and so he waited to see what the Democratic Convention would do. When the Democrats nominated Governor Woodrow Wilson, Brandeis knew what his course in the coming election would be.

Brandeis was convinced that Wilson cared profoundly about what was best for the American people. He was forthright, honest, free of party machines because he was a dark-horse candidate. As president of Princeton he had raised the standards of the university and brought a whole new spirit of scholarship to the campus. In his two years as governor of New Jersey he had defeated a political monopoly in Hudson County, reformed the election laws, established a public utility commission to regulate rates and improve service, and encouraged the legislature to pass a workmen's compensation law to provide payment to any workers injured on the job or those who contracted an illness as a result of the work they were doing.

Just what Brandeis had been fighting for all along: freedom from irresponsible monopolies in industry, public services, and in government. Wilson was his candidate. As soon as he and his family had had their month of August in South Yarmouth, he would take the stump for Wilson.

But his holiday on Cape Cod was interrupted by an invitation from Mrs. Woodrow Wilson, to have luncheon with her husband at their summer place in Sea Girt, New Jersey. Brandeis *would* interrupt his vacation to meet the candidate. His eyes sparkled as he set out to take an evening boat to New York and a morning train down to the Jersey shore. What would Wilson really be like? Some said he was a cold fish to shake hands with; others declared his Scottish sense of humor delightful. He was formal and stiff—no, he wasn't; he was easy to meet.

A refreshing sea breeze greeted him at Sea Girt, and at the governor's residence he took the hand of a gracious, fragile-seeming lady with golden brown hair and large brown eyes. A trace of the South in her speech reminded him of Kentucky. Ellen Axson Wilson was from Georgia. Governor Wilson was Virginia-born, and there was the same kind of Southern graciousness in his manner. He was formal, yes, but not stiff as Brandeis had been led to believe.

There were remarkable similarities between the

governor of New Jersey and the nationally known people's attorney. Both were tall, slender, handsome, correct and careful dressers, proper in their manners. Both wore glasses and had the same habit of speaking directly and bluntly.

Wilson wanted to consult Brandeis about the subject Brandeis understood better than any other man in America: how to regulate monopolies and trusts without destroying free enterprise. How can we prevent the abuses of private monopolies without creating government monopolies? Wilson needed the answer to that question, because he wanted to make the answer part of his campaign. Wise regulation by the government was perfectly possible, Brandeis told him, so that small businesses could compete with large, and so the public would not have to pay unreasonable prices for necessities.

"I don't want the American economy enslaved by a few wealthy czars," said Wilson, "but I don't want government regulation that will enslave us."

Brandeis agreed, and as soon as he returned to Massachusetts, he sent Mr. Wilson many of his private files to study. In addition he wrote out a long memorandum on the subject.

Woodrow Wilson began his campaign right after Labor Day, talking about a new freedom for the American people. Because of the help Brandeis had given him, Wilson was able to be entirely specific about how the new freedom was to be

achieved. It would require a new and stricter anti-
trust law among other things. A great deal of Brandeis's thinking became Wilson's, even the idea of
creating a federal trade commission to supervise fair
business practices.

Brandeis had faith in Wilson. He knew that one
day soon he would be able to talk to Wilson about
the need for a Jewish state in Palestine and about
his many other goals for the United States government. He went on a speaking tour in the Wilson-
for-President campaign.

Woodrow Wilson became President. His election, and the change from a Republican to a
Democratic administration, meant a great deal to a
great many. It would mean among other things that
the investigation of the New Haven would be re-
sumed, and in another year that battle finally won.

Of course, the election results started waves of
talk and speculation about cabinet appointments.
What appointment did President Wilson have in
mind for Attorney Brandeis? What was Brandeis
after? Most of the guessers guessed that he would be
appointed to a cabinet post: Attorney General, Secretary of Commerce or of Labor.

When reporters and even his friends asked,
"What about it, Mr. Brandeis?" he would simply
reply in his quiet manner, "Don't believe all you
hear."

Then something ugly began to happen, uglier

than he would have thought possible. A snowstorm
of letters descended upon President Wilson finding
fault with Brandeis, accusing him of having no integrity, no professional ethics. The President must
not consider appointing him to any position of trust.
It really grew into a smear campaign.

Brandeis knew he had enemies, and he knew
why. When a man took a stand on an issue, he
didn't expect everyone to be on the same side with
him. Boston's investment bankers and insurance men
feared him for his stand against money monopoly.
Many men in the legal profession considered him
too radical. The language of the campaign against
him grew steadily more shocking.

But some objections to him came from unexpected sources: a man who had been associated with
Brandeis in the Public Franchise League, the president of Harvard University, others who he had always thought were his friends. They were using
subtle and gross reasons to justify their objection to
Louis Brandeis in the President's Cabinet.

"I think I know the reason for that feeling,"
President Wilson wrote to an acquaintance in Boston. Brandeis knew too: he was Jewish. One magazine came right out and discoursed in print about
the "Jewish mind" when its operations are compli-
cated by altruism.

Brandeis had never been blind to obvious anti-

Semitism, but he hadn't realized—he truly hadn't realized—how many associates and acquaintances had that reservation about him. Of course, there had always been a few people who remained aloof from him and his family because they were Jewish, but on the whole his Boston and Cambridge friends and acquaintances had given no sign that they cared one way or the other. It was a saddening experience, but not one that he intended to dwell upon.

A time of trial brings real friends to the fore. Norman Hapgood of *Collier's Weekly* had supported him during many of his fights and had published many of Brandeis's articles on Wilson's campaign issues. Senator La Follette of Wisconsin was loud and clear in his praise of Brandeis and urged Wilson to appoint him. So did Felix Frankfurter, a young New York lawyer who had graduated from the Harvard Law School and was now in the Bureau of Insular Affairs. Six outstanding progressives of Boston including Edward Filene felt so outraged by the false accusations that they sent a long telegram to President Wilson, saying among other things, "We believe firmly that the great mass of men who voted for you in Massachusetts are wholeheartedly in favor of Mr. Brandeis as representing the fundamentals on which you were elected."

As a matter of fact, Wilson was very seriously considering Brandeis for his Cabinet. "I've got to have men in the Cabinet who have passed the acid test of honesty. Men who are brave. Men who are efficient. Men who have imagination," he had already said. And he particularly needed Brandeis's wide knowledge of finance and trusts. But the brand-new President yielded to his advisers and passed Brandeis by for the sake of party harmony. La Follette was heartbroken; Hapgood was "pretty blue." Louis Brandeis wrote a warmhearted letter of congratulation to James C. McReynolds when he learned that Wilson had appointed McReynolds as Attorney General.

In the months that followed, Brandeis willingly journeyed to Washington for consultations and conferences whenever the President needed him. Wilson listened to Brandeis's advice on making other appointments.

By the time the crisis over Wilson's Cabinet appointments had died down, Louis D. Brandeis was up to his chin in the Zionist movement. More than two years had passed since the garment strike and his first public declaration on Zionism. Since then he had become friendly with Jacob de Haas, the editor of the *Jewish Advocate* of Boston. Because De Haas was a newsman, he quite naturally met a great many prominent persons, and he had talked with Brandeis on other occasions about this issue or that. But it was the Wilson campaign that really brought De Haas and Brandeis together.

Jacob de Haas had visited with Brandeis at South Yarmouth that summer of 1912 for a conference about campaign tactics. Business completed, they talked of other things.

"Lewis Dembitz was a noble Jew," De Haas remarked of Brandeis's beloved uncle who had died in Louisville about five years before.

De Haas was himself an immigrant Jew, London-born, editor of the *London Jewish World* before he came to the United States. His consuming interest now was Zionism.

"I have been a Zionist since the day I met Theodor Herzl," he told Brandeis. "That was sixteen years ago."

They talked a long time about Zionism. Did De Haas know how Wilson felt about a Jewish state in Palestine? Yes, De Haas replied, he had already talked with the President about it, and Wilson was genuinely interested.

Louis Brandeis had already been converted to the idea of Zionism. His long conversation with Jacob de Haas inspired him to become active in the movement. Shortly after their visit at South Yarmouth, Brandeis joined the Federation of American Zionism, the group that later became the Zionist Organization of America. By the following spring he was traveling about the country, addressing Jewish groups on the importance and urgency of re-creating Palestine. To dwell on the ugly experience in prejudice he had just been through would have been negative. To work for a great dream was positive, forward looking, satisfying.

His first public appearance for Zionism was at the Plymouth Theatre in Boston on Sunday, March 30, 1913. The occasion was a mass meeting of Zionist sympathizers and those curious to discover what the movement was all about. The guest speaker was the European leader, Mr. Nahum Sokolow, a learned man who spoke many languages and was editor of *Hatsefirah* and general secretary of the Zionist organization in Europe. He reminded the audience of the many dreary centuries of suffering and frustration that the Jews had gone through, and called upon his listeners to make the dream of Palestine a living fact.

Like everyone else in the room Mr. Brandeis felt moved by the address, and moved to learn in the course of the conference that the first pioneers in Palestine had been struggling for nearly twenty years to create colonies in such places as Judea, Samaria, and Upper Galilee. More people were needed to make the barren land flourish.

When he himself rose, it was to make only a

short statement. He told the audience he had come
to announce his affiliation with the movement. "The
Jewish people have a great vision," he said, "and
they are known as the noblest nationality in the
world. In every land they are struggling for social
rights, and are trying to relieve the burden of their
friends and relatives in Russia, and to lessen the toil
of the poor. The great happiness in life is not to donate, but to serve. This great message that Herr Sokolow brought here for us may some day become a
reality, and the Jewish people may become a national state that they have aspired for and longed for
for a long time."

A little wave of excitement ran through the audience as he sat down. He was bringing them something fresh and new, telling them of their vision and
nobility, and in so very few words.

Louis Brandeis gave a full address in May to
the Young Men's Hebrew Association in Chelsea,
Massachusetts, on the theme, "We cannot afford to
do a mean thing." If the Jews were to go on being a
"priest people," to move out of the centuries of endurance and suffering into a new age of initiative
and self-reliance, their thinking, conduct, and planning must never be petty or even average.

Then he told them of an achievement by Professor Aaron Aaronsohn, who was head of the Jewish
Agricultural Experiment Station in Palestine: the

discovery in his laboratory of wild wheat. Botanists had been searching for years for a wheat that would grow in rugged, semi-arid places where the usual wheat could not survive. Professor Aaronsohn had emigrated from Romania to Palestine thirty-two years ago and had watched the Jewish population there grow to 150,000. Brandeis had given his audience a real measure of the potential: So many thousands in thirty-two years? What could not another thirty-two years bring!

Brandeis appeared in city after city, speaking to audiences that were largely Jewish, since it was they who must first be convinced of the need. He appealed particularly to Jewish leaders, to meetings of rabbis, teachers, business men and women, civic workers.

In 1913 the worst Jewish suffering was in Europe, and the center of the World Zionist movement was in Berlin. Brandeis was really calling upon American Jews to assist the European organization.

But Europe was spiraling down into war. Tensions had been gathering for years. Germany had been expanding her armies and her navy, frightening other European countries into an arms race. In June 1914 Archduke Francis Ferdinand, heir to the throne of Austria-Hungary, and his wife, were assassinated at Sarajevo, a Balkan town near the Serbian border. Austria-Hungary served an ultimatum upon

Serbia. Serbia was too small a country to defend herself, and she tried desperately to have the case heard by an international tribunal. But Austria-Hungary declared war on her, and troops began to move in other countries—in Russia and France. On August first, Germany declared war on Russia, then on France. When Germany marched troops through neutral Belgium to attack France, Great Britain declared war on Germany.

With Germany at war, Berlin could no longer be the center of World Zionism. The center must be moved to another continent.

Louis Brandeis, Jacob de Haas, and other Jewish leaders in America realized that they must assume the responsibility, that the movement must be directed from the United States—at least until World War I ended. So did Dr. Chaim Weizmann, head of the World Zionist Organization. He was at that time a university professor in England.

Two hundred American and European leaders came together in an emergency session at the Hotel Marseilles in New York City on the thirtieth of August, 1914, to find the answer to the question: What is the duty of American Zionists now? There were prominent persons present whom Louis Brandeis seldom saw, such as Nathan Straus, whose family owned the R. H. Macy store, with his flowing white beard; Henrietta Szold from Baltimore, daughter of a rabbi, founder of Hadassah; and Louis Lipsky of New York City, a man with a deep understanding of the situation in Europe. Dr. Schmarya Levin, Russian-born teacher, rabbi, writer, and lecturer, had come from Germany to represent the European group. He was a slight, gentle man with a neat moustache and small pointed beard.

Lipsky introduced Dr. Levin who explained the problem. Henrietta Szold appealed to the group to donate funds and services. Nathan Straus offered a hundred thousand dollars to American Zionists if they would assume the responsibility for directing the movement, and Jacob de Haas added his appeal.

Then the tall, slender people's attorney rose and addressed the group. Up to now not many had ever heard him speak. In a few short paragraphs and without melodramatics—just his self-contained courtroom calm—he told them he would join in the great work:

> *I have been to a great extent separated from Jews. I am very ignorant in things Jewish. But recent experiences, public and professional, have taught me this: I find Jews possessed of those very qualities which we of the twentieth century seek to develop in our struggle for justice and democracy; a deep moral feeling which makes them capable of noble acts; a deep sense*

*of the brotherhood of man; and a high intelli-
gence, the fruit of three thousand years of civilization.*

*These experiences have made me feel that
the Jewish People have something which should
be saved for the world; that the Jewish People
should be preserved; and that it is our duty to
pursue that method of saving which most promises success. . . .*

*By a sudden catastrophe, the movement
has been deprived of leadership by those who for
many years have successfully advanced it. . . .*

*To achieve our purpose we need the coop-
eration of everyone here and of the tens of
thousands whom those here can influence. Let
us work together! Carry forward what others
have, in the past, borne so well! Carry it forward to the goal for which we all long!*

When he finished, the audience sat in deep silence for several moments, until Jacob de Haas rose
to move that the meeting adopt a resolution creating
the Provisional Zionist Executive Committee, to assume responsibility for the Zionist movement. The
resolution was adopted, quickly and quietly, because
the meeting was now compelled by a single idea: to
elect a chairman of the new executive group, to
elect as its chairman this Daniel who had come

among them, this quiet-mannered and brilliant lawyer whom many had already begun to consider as a
successor to Herzl himself.

In another few moments Brandeis *was* chairman, and the sober meeting—where tensions had
been building in the August heat and humidity—was
on its feet, filling the room with applause that welled
up like a great wave of hope.

Chairman Brandeis organized the work of the
committee very soon afterward, in offices provided
by Nathan Straus. Everyone who worked with him
had to give his utmost, but it was never more than
the chairman did himself. "He has become the
leader for Jews living in the United States. His study
is a mecca for Jews of the United States and other
countries," said one of his associates.

He soon received a long letter from Chaim
Weizmann in England in which the World Zionist
leader said, "The American Provisional Executive
Committee should be given full power to deal with
all Zionist matters, until better times come."

Brandeis agreed absolutely. Palestine—the
whole Near Eastern area, in fact—was a pawn in the
war that was spreading over Europe and Asia
Minor. Palestine was part of the Turkish empire, and
the sultan of Turkey had joined the Central Powers:
Germany and Austria-Hungary. European sympathy
for the Zionist movement had been coming chiefly

from Great Britain, a leading Allied power. Palestine's whole situation was sensitive and dangerous. If the Central Powers lost the war, then the Turkish empire, including Palestine, would be carved up among the victors. If they won, what then?

What was happening right now to the Jewish colonies and the thousands of pioneers who had been striving to develop them for so many years? Intelligence reached Louis Brandeis and his committee that Jewish colonists were stranded behind the war curtain and suffering merciless persecution and starvation. As the war machines rolled over Asia Minor, destroying crops and cattle, everyone living there—Jew, Moslem, Gentile—faced utter famine.

The power of Louis Brandeis's leadership took effect immediately in mustering aid for Palestine. Hunger could not wait until governments and armies settled their differences; hunger was now.

Less than a month after Brandeis took office as head of the Provisional Committee, he and Schmarya Levin appeared at a big fund-raising meeting at Symphony Hall in Boston. There were over six thousand in the audience, and the *Jewish Advocate* called it a gathering of the most distinguished Hebrews ever witnessed in the area. Both men spoke. Brandeis with his clear, simple language moved the audience to tears with his theme, "Zionism and Patriotism." The men and women in the audience gave him seventy-five thousand dollars in twenty-five minutes.

By December Louis Brandeis and Dr. Levin had reached Springfield, Massachusetts, in their campaign, and on the first of January, 1915, they were addressing the United Zionist organizations of St. Louis at the Temple Israel on "The Duty of American Jews." All of these meetings received wide press coverage, and as a result each one was larger than the last. Brandeis extended his appeal to everyone—Catholics, Protestants, and Mohammedans —"in the name of God and humanity" to prevent the annihilation of the sufferers in the Holy Land. "A round half-million dollars must be raised by popular subscription at once, to charter and load an emergency relief ship, that shall be despatched to Palestine without unnecessary delay."

The first ship, the U. S. collier *Vulcan,* sailed from Philadelphia March 10 for Jaffa, carrying nine hundred tons of food. It would reach Palestine in time for the Passover. But that wasn't enough. The job wasn't yet done. Brandeis went on, speaking in Chicago, Cleveland, Providence, Portland, Maine, sometimes with Dr. Levin, sometimes with Jacob de Haas. At Columbia University in New York City, eight hundred filled all the seats, aisles, and doorways of Earl Hall to hear him. He gave them a frightening description of the condition of Jews in

Europe—in Belgium and Poland particularly—as well as in the Near East.

> *What a hoax of the justice of French liberalism! to have liberty, equality and fraternity submerged by the anti-Semitism of a few. . . . The reason we must make common cause with all the small nations of the world is that the large nations must surely come to the day when they will see that it isn't good national policy to suppress any one people and drive out of those people their national instinct. . . . The striving of a nation to express itself nationally has been the best work of democracy. Furthermore this should apply as well to the Jewish nation. . . . Zionism is an actuality. It is a potential force in Jewish life.*

Brandeis looked ahead to the day when the war would be over, when Zionists could once more work toward the creation of a Jewish state. He knew that President Wilson favored the idea, but the President had issued a proclamation of United States neutrality in the European war, and in 1915 he was struggling to maintain that neutrality. Peace had to be the next goal before the future of Palestine could be determined.

At the end of June of that year, the Federation

of American Zionists held its annual congress, or convention, in Boston. Louis Brandeis had roused so much interest in his one year as head of the Provisional Committee that twenty thousand attended that Sunday night, crowding and struggling into Mechanics Hall and filling the streets outside for a glimpse of him and a chance to hear him speak.

The hall was alive with American and Zionist colors. A portrait of Herzl, draped in blue and white, hung above the platform. "Without vision a people perish," said the rabbi who opened the meeting. There were four speakers, and when Louis D. Brandeis was finally introduced, the audience jumped to its feet, cheering wildly, waving hundreds of small Zionist flags in the air. The ovation went on and on, but at last they did let him speak.

> *I interpret your presence here as an expression of your faith; as testimony to your interest; as a promise to aid in carrying forward the Jewish ideals; as a determination to realize the Jewish hope of the twentieth century. . . . Stand up, each and every one of you, and be counted. Join the Zionist Organization and shoulder your part in this great movement. . . . Such is our duty as Jews and as Americans. By battling for the Zionist cause, the American ideal of democracy, of social justice and of liberty will be*

given wider expression. By such action the man-hood and womanhood of American Jews will be made manifest to the world. By concrete action, the prayer of twenty centuries will be made to come true. The great Herzl was right when he said in his Altneuland, *"If you wish it, it is no fable." Dreams may be made into realities.*

After the congress, one of the Boston papers said, "He is now the motivating power of a gigantic world movement."

Chapter 10

THE TRAGEDY OF PREJUDICE

"America has believed that each race had something of peculiar value which it can contribute to the attainment of those high ideals for which it is striving. . . . America has believed that in differentiation, not in uniformity, lies the path of progress. It acted on this belief; it has advanced human happiness, and it has prospered."

Louis Brandeis's influence was just as significant in the national capital. By the end of 1915, when he was raising the level of the Zionist movement to a new high, he had become a trusted adviser to President Wilson and other government people. Not only did they need his clear thinking and good judgment, but they had come to know him as a living library of information in a wide variety of fields: investments, banking, railroads, corporations, insurance, trusts, labor, and general economics. Sometimes they consulted him privately; sometimes he appeared before a committee to give its members the benefit of his specialized knowledge. Many realized how valuable he would be in a government position and regretted not having him in the Cabinet.

None realized his value more than President Wilson. When an opportunity opened up to bring Brandeis into the government, Wilson acted upon it.

The death of Associate Justice Joseph R. Lamar had created a vacancy on the United States Supreme Court, and the President must appoint his successor with the approval of the Senate. The names of many candidates were suggested to the President, most of them well qualified, and he gave them all a great deal of thought. The suggestion that he liked best came from Thomas W. Gregory, who had replaced McReynolds as Attorney General. When he had an opportunity to talk with the President, Gregory said, "I am going to make a suggestion, and I am going to ask you not to respond to it for a week. I am going to recommend Louis Brandeis for the Supreme Court. My reason is that he is one of the most progressive men in the United States, and equal to the best in learning and ability."

Wilson was delighted with the suggestion. He felt that the Court was too conservative, that it needed a progressive like Brandeis. But remembering the earlier fury about appointing Brandeis to the Cabinet, he moved cautiously. He first asked Gregory to find out whether Brandeis would accept such an appointment. Gregory soon reported back that Brandeis was willing to accept it.

In another few days the President sent a message to the Senate of the United States, which the clerk read aloud: "I nominate Louis D. Brandeis of Massachusetts to be Associate Justice of the Supreme Court of the United States, vice Joseph Rucker Lamar, deceased. Signed, Woodrow Wilson. The White House, 28 January, 1916."

The senators sat stunned for a moment, turning heads to look at one another in amazement. The President had consulted none of the party leaders, and the Senate must approve the appointment. "Impossible!" some of them sputtered when they found their voices. Newsmen in the press gallery scrambled to their phones.

Mr. Brandeis was in the national capital at the time, and when reporters rushed to him for a statement, he replied, "I have nothing whatever to say; I have not said anything and will not."

Headlines blazed in the newspapers, and the conservative *New York Sun* said bluntly:

First Jew Ever Picked for Bench
Long and Bitter Fight Expected in Senate
over Confirmation

It went on to call Brandeis "utterly and ridiculously unfit." *The New York Times* was more careful in its language, but its stand was clear: "Mr. Brandeis is essentially a contender, a striver after changes and reforms. The Supreme Court by its very nature is the conservator of our institutions." The *Boston Herald* and the *Boston Transcript* both came out against the appointment; so did the *Detroit Free Press*. But the *New York World* said with enthusiasm, "Because he is a radical of unusual ability and character . . . his elevation to the bench will be regarded by most people with emphatic approval." The *Springfield Republican* and the *Indianapolis Star* favored the appointment, as well as other important dailies.

Magazine comment soon followed. To Norman Hapgood, now editor of *Harper's Weekly*, Brandeis was a "great lawyer, a noble citizen and one of the bravest and most disinterested of men." The *Survey* hired a special worker to collect signatures on a petition asking the United States Senate to approve the appointment. The list was long and filled with important names.

President Wilson in his own words considered Brandeis "singularly qualified by learning, by gifts, and by character. . . . a friend of all just men and a lover of the right; and he knows more than how to talk about the right—he knows how to set it forward in the face of its enemies. . . ."

What is the United States Supreme Court? What does it mean to be appointed to the bench of that tribunal?

When George Washington, James Madison, Alexander Hamilton, and others assembled in Philadelphia in 1787 to write the United States Constitution, they designed a national government with three main branches: the legislative, to make the laws; the executive, to administer and enforce the laws; and the judicial, to interpret the law through a system of local, state, and federal courts. The highest court in the land, the last court to which a case may be appealed, is the Supreme Court of the United States. The Supreme Court determines whether a lower court has been right in its decision. It also determines whether laws passed by Congress and the states are constitutional. Its decisions are final and binding.

There are eight associate justices in the Supreme Court, and a chief justice who presides. They are appointed for life, so that they will be above any and all political pressures in making their decisions. An associate justice must be learned, wise, and fair. That is why the President must select him with great care and why the United States Senate must approve his nomination thoughtfully. To sit on the bench of the Supreme Court of the United States is to hold one of the most responsible and honored positions in the government.

It is hard today to understand why the nomination of Louis Dembitz Brandeis raised such a storm and why he was opposed by so many distinguished persons. The controversy raged for four months, and before it was over, just about everyone in America had become involved and had taken sides. Voters all over the country wrote to their senators, urging them to vote *for* Mr. Brandeis's nomination because he was liberal, honest, a man who loved the common people and wanted what was best for them; or *against* Mr. Brandeis's nomination because he was unethical as a lawyer, self-seeking, radical to the point of being a socialist, Jewish. The only valid argument against him came from the most conservative people who considered him too radical. Because his ideas were so many years ahead of his times, they were frankly afraid of him. Many who opposed him used the fact that he was Jewish for hate-mongering. But actually he was not the first Jew ever to be considered for the Supreme Court. As long ago as the 1850's President Millard Fillmore had wanted to nominate Judah P. Benjamin, but Mr. Benjamin had declined.

Alfred Brandeis wrote to congratulate his brother as soon as he heard of the nomination, and Louis replied, "I am not exactly sure that I am to be congratulated, but I am glad that the President wanted to make the appointment, and I am convinced, all things considered, that I ought to take it."

Alice cared less about the public fury than about her husband's personal happiness. He had been a free man for so many years that she wondered how he would bear being tied to a job. Still, he could not go on forever being a roving knight of the law; he was nearly sixty. "It is of course a great opportunity for service," she wrote to Alfred, "and all our friends here feel that he is the one man to bring to the Court what it greatly needs in the way of strengthening."

Elizabeth was still in college at the time. Susan had graduated the year before and was in Boston, working for the woman suffrage organization. They were not deeply affected by the debate over their father's nomination. They were accustomed to his being in the center of one public fight or another, and he always won in the long run. So they took the confirmation fight fairly calmly.

The United States Senate could not allow the controversy to solve itself in the newspapers. Its Judiciary Committee appointed a special subcommittee to hear both sides, weigh and sift the evidence, and then report to the Senate. The hearings that it conducted were formal, dignified, and fair. They began on February 9, 1916, and continued until the middle of March.

Prominent persons came to those meetings to make shocking accusations against Brandeis. A representative of Middle Western railroad interests stood before the committee to accuse Brandeis of "infidelity, breach of faith, and unprofessional conduct." Others claimed that in the New Haven case he had been deliberately engaged to wreck another railroad in which the New Haven was interested. And there were loud protests from the life insurance field, where he was still trying to get cheaper and better life insurance for working people.

The hearings were conducted very much like a trial with witnesses for both sides examined and cross-examined. Representing Mr. Brandeis and those who came to testify for him was his junior law partner, Edward McClennen. He assumed responsibility for gathering all the positive information and replies to accusations.

Brandeis made no public statements himself, but he worked hard behind the scenes to provide detailed data from his files and his remarkable memory.

A parade of character witnesses appeared in Louis Brandeis's behalf, many of them names that would grow more prominent in future years. Newton D. Baker, president of the National Consumers' League, was one, and, of course, Florence Kelley. Newsmen, always so well informed, came forward: the editor of *The Survey* and Norman Hapgood. Another was Walter Lippmann.

During February the subcommittee received a petition signed by fifty-five Bostonians asking the Senate not to confirm Brandeis's nomination. The most prominent name on that petition was the president of Harvard, A. Lawrence Lowell. "We do not believe that Mr. Brandeis has the judicial temperament and capacity which should be required in a judge of the Supreme Court. His reputation as a lawyer is such that he has not the confidence of the people." In reply to that, one of Brandeis's Boston law partners wrote to McClennen in Washington: "The fact the LDB has been and *is now* on the Committee of the Overseers to visit the Harvard Law School ought to be hammered in."

Soon a witness took the stand to accuse Brandeis of fraud in handling the family business of his own former partner Sam Warren. In 1889 Brandeis had assisted Sam Warren in drafting a contract to dispose of family properties. The Warren family was deeply disturbed and angered by the charge. They themselves wrote to state that one brother, Edward Warren, had later complained but that the rest of the family had always been very satisfied with the arrangement.

"It is not as unpleasant to us as would seem to the outside," Brandeis wrote to Alfred. "This attack continued throughout nine years has quite accustomed us to it, and we are glad to have it out. At all events the country including Boston will know what I have been 'up against.' I suppose eighteen centuries of Jewish persecution must have enured me to such hardships."

So many witnesses who appeared against him were discredited by careful cross-examination that Brandeis, his family and supporters, grew more hopeful that his nomination would be confirmed. But on the fourteenth of March seven former presidents of the American Bar Association presented a petition calling Brandeis "not a fit person to be a member of the Supreme Court of the United States."

At the top of the list appeared the name of former President William Howard Taft. There were at least two compelling reasons why Taft would oppose the appointment of Brandeis. First, he may have wanted the appointment himself; many of his friends had written to Wilson urging Taft's appointment. Second, a deep embarrassment still lingered in his memory of an investigation while he was President: the Ballinger-Pinchot affair, in which Brandeis had figured conspicuously.

Richard A. Ballinger had been Taft's Secretary of the Interior. His conservation policy had been challenged by Gifford Pinchot, chief of the United States Forest Service and Louis R. Glavis, the chief of the field agents in the Department of Interior. The challenge grew to serious accusations, because Ballinger had allowed private interests to buy public lands, some of them coal fields in Alaska. Taft upheld Ballinger and ordered Glavis removed. To Norman Hapgood, who was still editor of *Collier's Weekly,* it was news, and *Collier's* soon published an article, "The Whitewashing of Ballinger," by Louis R. Glavis. When Pinchot also criticized Ballinger to the United States Senate, Taft removed Pinchot. The article in *Collier's* and the resulting commotion in the newspapers forced a public hearing before a joint congressional committee. Louis Brandeis appeared at the hearings representing Mr. Glavis. Brandeis was able to place Ballinger in such a bad light that Ballinger had to resign to save the President of the United States from embarrassment. The whole episode had been politically damaging to Taft and had helped him lose the election to Wilson in 1912. Now, in a letter to a friend, Taft labeled Brandeis "a muckraker, an emotionalist for his own purposes, a socialist, prompted by jealousy, a hypocrite . . . utterly unscrupulous . . . Brandeis has adopted Zionism. . . . If it were necessary, I am sure he would have grown a beard to convince them that he was a Jew of Jews."

Brandeis and his friends realized that the petition from the American Bar Association could be most damaging. La Follette called the petitioners "hell-hounds" and "sleek respectable crooks," and he asked Louis Brandeis to prepare a brief or summary of the whole contents of the hearings for the final round of debate. "You know me and can trust me," La Follette assured him. "Take the hearings and make a brief for me just as if I was the man to be confirmed. Don't ask anybody else to do this. You do it—send it to me on plain paper typewritten without any signature."

Brandeis did. With his talent for clear analysis, he began to write, "The dominant reasons for the opposition to the confirmation of Mr. Brandeis are that he is considered a radical and is a Jew." There followed each charge that had been made against him, and his rebuttal. It was a careful, honest document, and exactly what his supporters needed.

The public hearings ended March fifteenth, and the subcommittee went into private session. On the first of April, Louis Brandeis happened to be in New London, Connecticut, when he received a telegram from Alice: "City editor of *Globe* says Washington advises confirmation 3 to 2." The subcommittee had upheld him. Now there would be more suspense until the Senate voted.

Meanwhile every possible final effort was made. Norman Hapgood invited friends to a social gathering at his Washington apartment on a Sunday evening to meet Louis Brandeis. Among them were some senators, and Hapgood watched with quiet satisfaction as they succumbed to Brandeis's winning personality.

President Wilson himself wrote to Senator Charles Culberson of Texas:

> *I named Mr. Brandeis . . . because I know him to be singularly qualified by learning, by gifts, and by character for the position. . . . I have tested him by seeking his advice upon some of the most difficult and perplexing public questions about which it was necessary for me to form a judgment. . . . I cannot speak too highly of his impartial, impersonal, orderly, and constructive mind, his rare analytical powers, his deep human sympathy, his profound acquaint-*

*ance with the historical roots of our institutions
and insight into their spirit, or of the many evi-
dences he has given of being imbued to the
very heart with our American ideals of justice
and equality of opportunity; of his knowledge of
modern economic conditions and of the way
they bear upon the masses of the people, or of
his genius in getting persons to unite in common and harmonious action and look with frank
and kindly eyes into each other's minds, who
had before been heated antagonists. This friend
of justice and of men will ornament the high
court. . . .*

Not until the twenty-fourth of May did the Judiciary Committee take its final vote and confirm the
nomination ten to eight. On the first of June the
United States Senate, upon hearing the recommen-
dation of the Judiciary Committee, voted its approval forty-seven to twenty-two.

Now a different kind of mail flooded in on the
Brandeis family—happy mail, jubilant mail, congrat-
ulating him.

On Monday morning, June 5, 1916, Alice Brandeis, her two daughters, her brother-in-law Alfred
Brandeis, and friends who had come forward to support Louis Brandeis during his days of trial, sat in
reserved seats in the Supreme Court chamber in the

Capitol. The Senate had once met in this room to hear the oratory of statesmen like Daniel Webster, Robert Hayne, and John C. Calhoun. Today it was filled with spectators, and so were the corridors outside.

Louis Brandeis rode from the Lafayette Hotel to the Capitol with Chief Justice Edward D. White. They went first to the robing room, where Louis Dembitz Brandeis put on the black robe of a justice. Then the nine members of the Supreme Court formed a line—the Chief Justice first, Associate Justice Brandeis last—and walked sedately through the hallway to the Court chamber.

A hush fell on the waiting spectators as they entered and filed to their places upon the rostrum—all but one. The newest justice waited at the clerk's desk. There he placed his left hand upon the Bible and raised his right as he repeated the oath of office:

> *I, Louis Dembitz Brandeis, do solemnly swear that I will administer justice without respect to persons, and do equal right to the poor and to the rich, and that I will faithfully and impartially discharge and perform all the duties incumbent upon me as Associate Justice of the Supreme Court of the United States, according to the best of my abilities and understanding,*

agreeable to the Constitution and the laws of the United States, so help me God.

Then he took his seat with the other eight.

Court closed for the summer then and would not reopen until October. Louis Brandeis and his family went to South Yarmouth for a quiet, restful summer.

He did go to Philadelphia in July for the annual congress of the Zionists. When he appeared upon the platform, the ovation he received was deafening. At adjournment the entire meeting rose and began to move toward him in such a great crush that he had to leave by way of a fire escape.

To all the congratulations, love, and happy triumph, he replied with a low-voiced gentle, "Thank you."

Chapter 11

WHAT A LOVABLE LAND

*"The land is an inspiration to effort.
. . . The Palestine Development
Council is only an instrument for
doing things. The thing that it
plans to do is not to extend charity,
but to create opportunities for people worthy of Palestine to upbuild
and develop it."*

Justice and Mrs. Brandeis moved to Washington in October, taking an apartment in the Stoneleigh Courts building at Connecticut Avenue and L Street, not far from the White House. They furnished it in their usual plain and simple way— nothing costly, nothing for show. A second apartment, on the other side of the building, was Justice Brandeis's office.

Almost any other man under the circumstances would have thought in terms of renting or buying a mansion-sized house in keeping with his new status. But Louis and Alice Brandeis were so accustomed to living frugally that they saw no reason to change.

Their house in Otis Place had always been rented, because he did not like to own property. There was no problem about giving it up.

They would be by themselves a great deal of the time. Elizabeth still had another two years at Radcliffe and would be with them only for the holidays. Susan had graduated from Bryn Mawr and was studying law at the University of Chicago. Shortly after her enrollment she received an exciting package in the mail: her father's own books from his law-school days.

He had arranged to withdraw from his law firm. It became Dunbar, Nutter & McClennen. Justice Brandeis did not take any of the staff members of his Boston law office to Washington with him, much to the disappointment of several. Instead, he engaged as his law clerk a Harvard Law School graduate, chosen for him by Felix Frankfurter who had become a professor there. For the past several years Professor Frankfurter had been picking a new law clerk each year for Justice Holmes from among the top of the graduating class at the Law School. The lucky young man—the first was Calvert Magruder— would gain priceless behind-the-scenes experience in the workings of the Supreme Court. Magruder eventually became a United States Circuit Court judge himself. Many of Justice Brandeis's young secretaries in Washington went on to positions of prominence.

The national capital was full of tensions and excitement in the fall of 1916. Not only was Wilson coming up for reelection, but the war in Europe had grown to such dangerous proportions that it was having a deep impact on the American economy and politics. The warring nations were buying supplies in America and creating a false prosperity. Americans were growing more and more pro-Ally in their feelings, and Wilson and his Cabinet were finding neutrality harder and harder to maintain as German submarines prowled the seas, sinking British ships and often killing American passengers aboard them.

Public opinion in the United States divided into two camps: those who wanted America to enter the war and those who wanted her to remain neutral.

By election time in November the war was the number-one campaign issue. The vote was heavy. Wilson went back in by a very narrow margin.

As a member of the Supreme Court, Justice Brandeis could not participate in the election campaign, but he wanted Wilson to remain in office. He saw in Wilson a man of real vision, and he saw in Wilson's dream of a world government the hope of all small nations when the war finally ended. The President had already outlined his ideas for a League of Nations: "An association of the nations, all bound together for the protection of the integrity of each." Palestine could be one of those nations if the Allies won the war.

But they weren't winning—not that year. The German war machine seemed invincible. Soon the Kaiser gave orders to wage unrestricted submarine warfare on all shipping. Headlines blazed in the American papers; excitement mounted and war talk spread. When the shocking knowledge came to light that Germany was trying to make a military alliance with Mexico, American indignation rose to fever pitch. Wilson went into a long conference with his Cabinet. Then, on April 2, 1917, he appeared before both houses of Congress and asked for a declaration of war against Germany. House and Senate concurred with large majorities.

Justice Brandeis was already an unofficial consultant to the President and many of the President's closest aides. "A talk with Brandeis always sweeps the cobwebs out of one's mind," Wilson had said. An amazing assortment of persons came to Brandeis for just that purpose. Now that the United States was at war, they would come to him with the gravest burdens of their lives. He was a good listener, noting everything the person had to say. Sometimes he said nothing in reply, letting the visitor find his own answer by talking out his problem. Now, in this extraordinarily tragic year of war, Brandeis made an extraordinary decision: to remain in Washington all summer so that he would be available to anyone who wished to seek his advice.

His wife and his daughter Elizabeth and their lifelong friend Mrs. Evans spent most of the summer in the Dedham house. Susan took a war job in Washington. The Justice did manage short vacations at South Yarmouth during the war, but most of his summers were spent in the national capital.

Brandeis particularly cherished the opportunity to work with the President and the President's closest friend and aide, Colonel Edward House, in outlining possible terms of a future peace treaty. He was especially able to help them on the situation in the Near East, because he kept in touch by cable with Chaim Weizmann and other Zionist leaders in Europe.

The   Near   East—Palestine,   Jordan,   Syria,

Lebanon—was occupied by German and Turkish troops when the United States entered the war. General Edmund H. H. Allenby of the British Expeditionary Force was in command of the Allied campaign there. He was conducting a slow and careful military advance that gave real promise of victory.

That same spring Great Britain's Foreign Minister, Arthur James Balfour, arrived in the United States. Tall, with a shock of white hair and a white moustache, Balfour was an experienced statesman who had once been Prime Minister. With him came a group of specialists, Army and Navy officers, and other men concerned with Britain's war program, to consult with President Wilson and others responsible for America's war program. Military victory would be only the first step. After that England, France, the United States, and other Allies would virtually have to re-create the map of Europe and the Near East. The defeated countries, demoralized by the war, would be unable to do it themselves. Countries that had been ruled by the Turks for hundreds of years would be left with no government at all.

Balfour favored the idea of a Jewish Palestine as a British protectorate, and an Allied victory would make this possible. He had already talked with Chaim Weizmann in London about the Palestine question, and when at last he met Brandeis at a White House luncheon, he clasped the justice's hand

and said, "You are one of the Americans I had wanted to meet."

Like countless others before him, Balfour was deeply impressed with Brandeis's idealism and his straightforward approach to the subject of Zionism. They met twice more before Balfour returned to England: at breakfast at Balfour's hotel, and later at the British Embassy. "I am a Zionist," Balfour commented at one point.

In the weeks following Balfour's departure Louis Brandeis kept in touch with Chaim Weizmann in England, who was in touch with the British government. The heat and humidity of Washington seemed utterly unimportant to the justice as he drove persistently toward an exciting result: the famous Balfour Declaration.

Chaim Weizmann soon cabled a preliminary draft to Washington, which had been tentatively approved by the British Foreign Office. Brandeis and Colonel House consulted with Stephen Wise and Jacob de Haas. They suggested some further revisions. Their text went through still more revisions in London, and on November 2, 1917, Lord Balfour issued the final version in behalf of his government:

His Majesty's Government view with favor the establishment in Palestine of a National Home for the Jewish people, and will use their best endeavors to facilitate the achievement of this object, it being clearly understood that nothing shall be done which may prejudice the civil and religious rights of the existing non-Jewish communities in Palestine or the rights and political status enjoyed by Jews in any other country.

The prayer of twenty centuries was coming true. "If you wish it, it is no fable," the great Herzl had said. Dreams may be made into realities.

On December 9, 1917, General Allenby and the British Expeditionary Force entered Jerusalem, their liberation of the Holy Land complete.

Not until July of the next year did the war in Europe show real signs of coming to an end—in the heat and mud of the Second Battle of the Marne. The German people themselves were sick of war and starvation; their morale was cracking. Austria-Hungary was on the brink of collapse, her people and economy utterly exhausted. At last the smoldering revolution inside of Germany burst forth, and the Kaiser was forced to abdicate. It meant surrender. The killing ceased on November 11, 1918.

Once the guns were silent, the terms of peace could be written, and all the hopes of every sort of people everywhere could begin to rise. Many small countries—like Palestine—which had been under the rule of one foreign power or another, hoped for a new identity.

Louis Brandeis, Stephen Wise, Jacob de Haas in

the United States, Chaim Weizmann in England, Nahum Sokolow on the Continent, and many other Jewish leaders had been doing their planning since the announcement of the Balfour Declaration. Weizmann had gone to Palestine early in 1918 to see for himself just how bad the conditions were that they would have to start with.

Justice Brandeis had written a five-point code for Palestine: equality for all regardless of race, sex, or faith; equality of opportunity; all public lands to be leased on terms that would insure fullest development; cooperatives for agriculture, industry, commerce, and finance; free public education. The Zionist congress in Pittsburgh in 1918 had adopted his code and sent it on to those who would present the Zionist plea to the Paris Peace Conference.

The purpose of the Paris Peace Conference—to begin in January—was to write a treaty that would end the war permanently. It would decide the future of the defeated countries, determine where new boundaries were to be drawn, which small countries would have independence, what areas would have to be occupied by the Allies' armies until they could look after themselves. It would have to think of starving and dislocated populations and ruined cities. Men like Woodrow Wilson wanted a merciful, intelligent treaty that would restore the ruined economies and make possible a permanent world peace.

Others wanted vengeance, punishment of those who had begun the war. The conference would be under such pressures of greed and generosity, vengeance and compassion, with each nation's representatives jockeying for favor and position, that many wondered how much it could really accomplish. It would obviously need a leading personality of superhuman fortitude to control it. More than one person could imagine Justice Brandeis in that role.

"The essential items of the peace would be economic," said Alvin Johnson of the *New Republic* magazine. "I wanted Louis D. Brandeis to head our delegation. Brandeis was our greatest lawyer, our profoundest practical economist, a wise man who knew the past and could foresee the future." So convinced was Johnson that he interviewed Mr. Brandeis on the subject.

The Supreme Court justice shook his head. The men at the peace conference would be in the position of gods, he said. They could give the world universal peace or universal chaos. "I am not a candidate for the position of a god," he told Johnson.

President Wilson himself headed the American delegation that went to Paris, to meet with the delegates from twenty-six other nations around a horseshoe-shaped table in the Salle de la Paix (Hall of Peace) in the Ministry of Foreign Affairs. The four countries with the greatest influence at the conference were the United States, France, Great Britain, and Italy.

During that winter and spring of 1918–1919 the Supreme Court kept Justice Brandeis busy, but he was in close touch all of the time with what went on in Paris. Anxiously he read every bulletin, every cable, every news release, realizing how earnestly President Wilson was working to make a League of Nations covenant part of the terms of the peace treaty. And he knew, too, that President Wilson wanted the treaty makers to grant Great Britain a trusteeship over Palestine.

In February the Council of Ten—the central executive group of the peace conference—granted an audience to five Jewish leaders, each of whom spoke for five minutes to plead for a Jewish national homeland in Palestine. Lord Balfour was present to hear them. When Chaim Weizmann spoke, he defined the Jewish national home as, "The creation of an administration which would arise out of the natural conditions of the country—always safeguarding the interests of non-Jews—with the hope that by Jewish immigration Palestine would ultimately become as Jewish as England is English."

The general reaction of the council was sympathetic. The French delegate announced that France would not object to the formation of a Jewish state. But the tensions and pressures at the peace conference were staggering. The delegates were so involved with demobilizing armies, redesigning the map of Europe, debating disarmament, reparations, and the League of Nations, that the whole problem of what to do about the Near Eastern lands—the wreckage of the Turkish empire—had to be set aside.

Louis Brandeis and Jacob de Haas talked often and worried together about the whole complex situation, as the Paris peace talks dragged on into April and May. Brandeis knew that if he were there he might be able to accomplish something. He wanted to meet such men as Weizmann, to talk face to face with the diplomats of Great Britain and France— with Lord Balfour in particular.

"And I want to see Palestine for myself," he said.

He wanted to make his own observation of conditions and learn at first hand which reports were true, which false. How were the colonies really faring? What did they need? And there was the compelling beauty of the land that must be seen to be believed.

Why not? He discussed it with Alice, with De Haas and others, and the decision was easy. As soon as the Supreme Court closed for the summer, he would go. De Haas would go with him, but Alice would not. They both felt that she was not sturdy enough for the wartime conditions they were bound to run into. Europe was still in an unsettled state; trains and hotels would give poor service, if any; and Palestine was under military rule.

But Susan would go as far as London. She had completed her law studies and had just received her degree from the University of Chicago. A mature woman by now, plainly dressed like her mother, she went aboard the *Mauretania* with him in June.

They were both deeply excited about the trip. She had never been abroad before; except for one short business trip, he had not set foot in Europe since his student days in Dresden. Susan was frankly disappointed that she would not see Paris or Palestine, but there would be another year. She understood that her father was on an important mission, not a holiday, and he must go on without her.

Their ship docked in Southampton on the southern coast, and from there they took a train up to London. One of the first glimpses they caught of the historic city was from the train window—the tall square tower of Parliament with its clock and famous bell, Big Ben, which tolls out the hours. A mist blurred the buildings around its base. As soon as they were settled in Claridge's Hotel, Justice Brandeis wrote a happy letter to his wife. London was civilization, he told her. "London is living. All the horrors of bigness are absent." They were stopping

at one of the most gracious hotels in one of the loveli-
est sections of the city, at Grosvenor Square, near
the formal landscaping of Hyde Park and Kensing-
ton Gardens.

When he went on to Paris and Palestine, Susan
would remain with Mrs. De Haas. Understanding
Susan's disappointment at being left behind, Mrs.
De Haas planned a tour for both of them through
Scotland and the Lake District in northern England
—the scenic region made famous by the Lake Poets:
Coleridge, Wordsworth, and Southey.

Brandeis's influence and wisdom were so in demand that almost at once he attended a meeting of a
London Zionist group called the Actions Committee
Conference. There he met Chaim Weizmann, a
heavy-set man, not as tall as himself, balding, with a
neatly barbered moustache and chin whiskers. Brandeis experienced a mixture of relief and disappointment after exchanging a few ideas with Weizmann.
The latter was not the rascal that his enemies
painted him; neither was he so great as his followers
claimed. Weizmann felt some secret coolness toward
Brandeis's Puritanical manner and found that Brandeis's "scrupulous honesty and implacable logic"
made him hard to work with. These two men would
experience much deeper disappointment in each
other in the years ahead, and the Zionist movement
would suffer for it.

Brandeis and De Haas remained in London only two days before taking a boat across the English Channel to France and a train up to Paris. The work of the peace conference was over, the text of the treaty to be signed at the Palace of Versailles completed. It did contain a covenant for the League of Nations; but a later treaty with defeated Turkey would decide the fate of Palestine.

Most of the delegates to the conference were still in Paris, so that Brandeis was able to consult with President Wilson, Lord Balfour, and French and Italian statesmen. He particularly wanted to talk to the Zionist representatives who would continue the effort to obtain a Palestine mandate and plan the new nation's government and economy.

"Be particularly careful," he warned them, "not to let a few capitalists get control of the natural resources for their own private gain." He did not want money monopolies to come in and take over large tracts of land, water rights, and whatever other natural riches there might be. They would drain the economy for profits before it could even get started.

But the real purpose of his being abroad was to see Palestine for himself, to find out how serious the starvation and suffering were. So far, Jewish adventurers had founded more than forty colonies in Palestine. Had they all survived?

Because the Near East was under military occupation, Justice Brandeis and Jacob de Haas had to enter Palestine by way of Egypt. From Marseilles on the southern coast of France they took a steamer, the *Malwa*, across the Mediterranean Sea. The water was a brilliant, glistening, bright blue, the air clear, the sky cloudless. Louis Brandeis took time during the voyage to write a note to his wife describing the vivid scene, assuring her that he would one day bring her here.

Both men were experiencing a strong sense of doing something profoundly important, of moving into the midst of a great historic event. As the *Malwa* approached the coast of Africa and turned her bow toward Port Said, they could see the activity on the docks, the soldiers on duty. Port Said stood out on a peninsula at the entrance to the Suez Canal. At that time many British officials were in the Egyptian capital, Cairo, as well as British and American consuls. So, before proceeding to Palestine, the travelers went to Cairo to meet diplomats and army officers. Egyptian Zionists gave the two Americans a warm reception.

Brandeis and De Haas were learning how intensely all of these small countries wanted their independence. Egypt in particular was tired of being a British protectorate. She had been under British rule for more than thirty years. The men recalled that representatives from Syria had come to the Paris

Peace Conference, asking for national independence at the same time that the Zionists had. If Palestine failed, the other small countries around her might fail, too.

At long last, after the military red tape had been cleared, Brandeis and his companions boarded a train on the special military railroad which the British had built to haul troops and supplies across the desert of Sinai to Jerusalem. The cars, bareboned and plain, had been standing in the subtropical sun, but the two men were glad to be on their way. When the train reached the Suez Canal, the passengers had to get out with all their belongings and climb into a truck which jostled and bumped across a drawbridge floating on pontoons. On the other side there was more red tape with passports and army permits.

Another train pulled in and they climbed aboard to jounce along all night. At dawn they reached Gaza, ancient town of the Philistines. It meant that they were approaching the southern end of Palestine. The countryside was rolling, sandy, like the American Southwest. As daylight increased, the colors outside grew more vivid—yellow, burnt orange, green; brilliant red blooms; vivid blue sky. Their next stop was Lod, or Lydda, where they changed again. The next train took them east by south to Jerusalem. It climbed continually, winding among the rocks of the central mountain range toward the ancient Holy City high up in the interior.

As the altitude increased the travelers found themselves passing through green forest, then higher up the world outside the window was barren rocks, some gray, some muted orange—sudden rises, steep slopes—and above it all, the scalding sun in a sky hazed by dust.

The old city of Jerusalem is a walled town of yellow sandstone that gleams like gold when the sun is low. Two main streets beginning at the Jaffa Gate on the west and the Damascus Gate on the north intersect in the middle. Otherwise it is a labyrinth of narrow crooked streets—some dead-end, some completely vaulted over by the buildings. It is entirely of stone. Like every other ancient walled city, a new section has spread out beyond the wall, over the hills and dales to the western side.

The train pulled in to a station about three quarters of a mile outside the city, and from there the hot and weary travelers went by car through the Jaffa Gate to the Grand New Hotel, where the standard joke was that it was neither grand nor new. But Justice Brandeis and his friend were not there to seek tourist comforts in a region that had just lived through five years of warfare.

Because Brandeis was one of the most influential Zionists in the world, a man to whom the President of the United States turned frankly for advice, he was a living hope to every Zionist in Palestine. An elaborate program of receptions, meetings, and guided tours in this most historic of regions awaited him.

One of his earliest sight-seeing ventures was to the Mount of Olives, a rise of land just east of Jerusalem, where David of the Old Testament had taken refuge, and where Jesus of the New had experienced his Ascension. On its western slope is the Garden of Gesthemane, where Judas betrayed Jesus to the Romans.

Louis Dembitz Brandeis stood on top of the Mount of Olives and saw the town of Bethlehem down among the hills to the south. Eastward lay the vivid blue water of the Dead Sea. Northward the fertile green ribbon of the Jordan River Valley marked the course of the river as it ran from the Sea of Galilee to the Dead Sea. To the west he could make out the Mediterranean. Civilization here went back so far in time! It meant so much to so many!

Profoundly moved by all that he saw, he turned to a companion and said in a voice husky with emotion, "What a lovable land!"

Another of his planned tours took him, De Haas, and others to a typical Jewish colony—Zichron Jacob—just south of Mount Carmel. The village had been founded thirty-seven years ago. Its whitewashed-stone and red-roofed houses clustered along the main street. The visitors met with the unpaid members of the village council, saw the vegetable gardens and fruit orchards, sensed the deeply democratic spirit of the whole community.

But Brandeis and De Haas were arriving at the same point in their thinking at the same time. This was an *ideal* situation. Before leaving home, they had received funds of information about the persecution, starvation, and sacrifice in many of the colonies. How could they get away from their guides and escorts and see the grim truth? How did Palestine look when it did not wear gala? How did the colonists live when not on parade? was how De Haas put it.

They rented an old Ford, hired a guide named Pesach, and set out with camping gear, water, and food to the northward, through the plain of Sharon which lies along the Mediterranean, north of the present city of Tel Aviv. Pesach was a goatherd who whistled his goatherder's call as he drove them along in a zigzagging course. They could not have found their way alone. There was not even a footpath to mark the course over the gray-white ridges of land. Occasional camel tracks told them that others had traveled this way. Wild plants wilting in the scorching sun reminded them that it was the dry season, that this arid land would need a great deal of modern irrigation before it would prosper and bear. Occasionally the sight of a broken-down and deserted army truck reminded them of the war just ended and the peace not yet written. Foot soldiers had slogged over these barren slopes.

They did come upon a sign of life as they approached the region of Galilee. Several colonists were pulling a harvester with a team of horses, taking it to their settlement in Lower Galilee. They were about to make camp for the night and invited the travelers to join them.

Justice Brandeis shook his head and thanked them. He wanted to go on farther while there was still daylight.

"Darkness comes suddenly here," they warned him.

When the colonists understood his mission, they advised him to turn eastward toward Mount Tabor and to pass it on its southern side. He thanked them, accepted some drinking water, and he and De Haas rode on. They saw Mount Tabor in the distance very soon afterward, a great dome with wooded sides. Pesach guided the Ford along goat tracks up the gradual slopes past the Mount.

Suddenly ahead of them gleamed the bright blue water of the Sea of Galilee. "A thrilling sight in a land of drought," De Haas wrote of it later.

They jounced on, still gaining altitude, until

they stopped to look at a crudely fashioned monument, the memorial to an unknown Jewish soldier. Both men got out of the car and stood with uncovered heads for a moment, reading the Hebrew legend:

NEFTER PELONI SHOMER YISROEL

"Hurry!" said Pesach.

They obeyed, and the car struggled on up and around the curving rocky course. An armed and mounted guard, a shomer, ordered them to stop, but as soon as they had proved their identity, he allowed them to pass. But first, to make them understand their danger, he bade them look down into the valley. There just below them was a cluster of Bedouin tents. Bedouins are a nomadic people, Moslem in faith and hostile to the idea of a Jewish nation.

They drove on until another shomer challenged them. They were approaching the village of Poreah, he told them. "Be extremely careful if they do not expect you." This was what they had come to see— the grim side of life in a colony that did not expect them.

Darkness was settling fast as they drove past cultivated fields toward the cluster of cottages. Citizens on guard duty stopped them, then took them to the home of Louis Goldman.

Louis Goldman had died a while ago, and Justice Brandeis and Jacob de Haas visited with his widow and son. They sat together on the porch of the cottage, looking at the River Jordan in the distance as it glistened in the moonlight. Justice Brandeis listened to a detailed chronicle of Poreah. Louis Goldman had come from St. Louis years ago to found this colony with financial help from those back home. But the support from St. Louis had failed, and the war had reduced them to poverty. Now they were even in doubt about their crops. It was a tragic story, yet Brandeis heard no mention of giving up.

When young Goldman told him that twelve Shomerim were waiting at Semach to escort him on the next part of his journey, Brandeis asked, "Why? How do they know?"

"We did not expect you. We did not even know you were in this part of the country, until an hour ago word reached us from Semach. . . . My brother-in-law Schochet is their leader, and he sent the message."

Brandeis then asked, "Do we need an escort? And, if so, we are the guests of the British government, and we shall ask the military governor at Semach to provide it."

"I am sure you will not so dishonor us."

Of course, he intended no dishonor. Traveling

with Shomerim deepened his understanding of the importance of everything that was happening here.

The two explorers reappeared finally at the Grand New Hotel, weary, dusty, but richer as a result of all they had seen and experienced.

Louis Brandeis and Jacob de Haas returned to America in time for the twenty-second convention of Zionists, held in Chicago in September 1919. It was now called the Zionist Organization of America. Four thousand attended.

Even though the Treaty of Sèvres between the Allies and Turkey, giving Great Britain a mandate over Palestine, would not be a legal fact for nearly a year, the conference was vibrant with confidence. So many plans had gone forward for the administration of the new nation—for the planting of vineyards and orange groves, for immigration, irrigation, colonization, education, building of roads and industry, even the creation of cities—that it already seemed like a reality.

Justice Brandeis sat on the platform with De Haas and other outstanding leaders at one of the general sessions, waiting to give a report on his trip. The excitement of the conference was contained until another speaker made a reference to Louis Brandeis as our "great silent leader." Every man and woman in the big, crowded room rose and cheered until they cried. When the outburst subsided, they sang the Jewish national anthem, "Hatikvah" ("Our Hope").

From the overcharged atmosphere in Chicago, Brandeis returned to the quiet life that he and Alice lived in Washington, and to his fourth winter with the United States Supreme Court.

Chapter 12

THE SUPREME COURT YEARS

"*Experience should teach us to be most on our guard to protect liberty when the government's purposes are beneficent. Men born to freedom are naturally alert to repel invasion of their liberty by evil-minded rulers. The greatest dangers to liberty lurk in insidious encroachment by men of zeal, well-meaning, but without understanding.*"

The Sunday afternoon teas that Justice and Mrs. Brandeis held were probably their biggest social events. The teas became famous. High-ranking diplomats, humble folk, old and young, hurried to them eagerly for an opportunity to have a few minutes' conversation with the justice. Alice Brandeis was both gracious and strict, steering as many as possible to a short audience with her husband. He had so much to give to others in the way of ideas and inspiration that every moment of the afternoon was precious. For his own part he especially enjoyed the young people who came, particularly Elizabeth's college friends. They were the most stimulating, the most open-minded, with their eyes focused not on the past but on the distant horizon.

Alice Brandeis's dinner parties were for smaller groups of men and women, those with whom the justice wanted to talk in a relaxed atmosphere: specialists in fields like labor relations or child welfare, congressmen, and members of the press. They all came knowing their courage would be increased for whatever battle they were waging during the day.

The justice was sixty-four in 1920, his hair white, and his energy must be conserved for the next day's work on the bench. And so Alice was strict with these guests, too, no matter how notable. Should any of them linger until ten, Alice rose and graciously suggested that the evening had come to an end.

The man with such a brilliant mind, who filled others with so much courage and inspiration, who was so farsighted and forward-looking, never accepted the automobile. Cars had begun to appear on the roads and in the streets of cities like Boston and Washington in increasing numbers during the last ten years, but Justice Brandeis continued to enjoy his big-wheeled, horse-drawn carriage on outings into Potomac Park, until by 1923 it simply became too dangerous for himself and the horse.

He never did learn to drive a car. Elizabeth learned, and eventually did the driving for her parents. Mrs. Brandeis decided that they needed a car in the country and bought a Model-A Ford. Later she purchased a V-8.

The country for them by then was in Chatham, an old historic whaling town far out on Cape Cod. They had rented a cottage there for the first time in 1922 and liked the place so well they went there every summer. In 1924 the justice bought the house they were renting on the small tidal river, Oyster Creek, when the owner decided to sell.

Justice Brandeis's mind remained clear and keen until he was well past eighty. He served as a Supreme Court justice for twenty-three years. During that time he wrote 528 opinions, many of them on highly technical subjects, such as patents and copyrights, banking, and the economics involved in public utilities and labor questions.

Upon the other eight men in the Supreme Court he had a strong influence over the years. Even when they disagreed with him, they felt a profound respect for him. They were not always the same eight. At the time of his appointment, the chief justice was Edward D. White, over seventy, a conservative from Louisiana, who had served in the Confederate Army and was the first Southerner in the Supreme Court since the Civil War. Joseph W. McKenna, a Philadelphian, also in his seventies, was even more conservative than White, and so were William Rufus Day of Ohio and Willis Van Devanter of Wyoming.

But John Hessin Clarke, one of the younger men and a Wilson appointee, proved to be a liberal who often stood with Brandeis in the court's decisions. The oldest member of the bench was the youngest in his thinking when Brandeis came to the Supreme Court. That man was Oliver Wendell Holmes. He was then seventy-five, and had been appointed by President Theodore Roosevelt fourteen years before.

Brandeis and Holmes had admired one another ever since their first meeting through Sam Warren nearly thirty-eight years earlier. During his Boston years, Brandeis had often met Holmes at the Parker House, a hotel near the courts, for beer and a talk. Holmes had heard Brandeis argue such cases as those involving maximum hour and minimum wage laws of Oregon. Now that they were both on the bench, their relationship took on a very special quality. They did not always agree, but their opinions, particularly their dissenting opinions, would be a forecast of the trend in American law.

The Supreme Court is the highest and final protector of human rights in the United States. The nine men who make up that tribunal render decisions by rule of the majority. At least five justices must agree. The opinion or opinions of the other four—the dissenting opinions—are just as valuable and important, because they are often years ahead of their time. On occasion the Supreme Court has reversed its own position after many years have passed, finally giving as a majority opinion an idea that was once a dissent. For instance, the Supreme Court once upheld the idea of the all-white primary which in some states prevented the Negro from voting. Less than ten years later it reversed itself, declaring such a law unconstitutional. The liberal dissenting opinions of Holmes and Brandeis in a conservative period of American history were forecasts of the future. And they influenced the future, because law students read them as part of their training.

"Oliver Wendell Holmes and Louis Dembitz Brandeis have achieved a spiritual kinship that marks them off as a separate liberal chamber of the Supreme Court. On the great issues that go down to the fundamental differences in the philosophy of government these two are nearly always together; often they are together against the rest of the court." Thus wrote a newsman in the *St. Louis Post-Dispatch*. "The memorable dissents of Holmes and Brandeis in cases involving the rights of the individual—human rights as against property rights —have been to liberals as a cup of water in a desert."

The newsman was referring to the labor movement and to the fact that both Holmes and Brandeis believed labor unions had a right to organize and bargain for their members. In the early days of the labor movement, many learned men believed that this violated the property rights of the manufacturer or miner. Both Holmes and Brandeis realized that America was expanding so rapidly that her economy was suffering from growing pains and maladjustments. Government was democratic, but business and industry were not; and so, the government, through good laws, must make industry more democratic by allowing unions to organize. In other words, both men believed that law must keep up with the times and relate to life.

Justice Brandeis was still the hard-working dynamo, but he was careful of his health. If he felt mentally tired, he lay down and napped for fifteen or twenty minutes, or went out into the fresh air for a walk or drive.

All of his law clerks—the young men whom Professor Frankfurter sent him from the Harvard graduating class each year—testified to his thoroughness and accuracy. According to Dean Acheson, his third assistant, Justice Brandeis's standard for work was "perfection as a norm, to be bettered on special occasions."

One day young Acheson made a mistake that stopped the justice at the last minute from delivering a scheduled opinion. When Mr. Brandeis returned to his office, he handed his assistant two bound volumes of reports and asked, "Did you read all the cases cited in the footnotes?" Acheson said he had. "Suppose you read these two again." Acheson discovered that he had passed through two which had nothing to do with the case being heard. "Please remember that your function is to correct my errors, not to introduce errors of your own," Justice Brandeis told him.

The justice wrote out his opinions in longhand, instead of dictating them to a stenographer. Then followed revision after revision. He used different colored pencils so that his assistant could keep track of the corrections. The final draft went to the printer to be set in type.

Often the opinions that he wrote were a continuation of the history he had begun to create years ago. So many grew out of the social problems of the times!

One was the case of the yellow-dog contract. That was an agreement in which the worker promised not to join a union while he worked for the company. In this instance the Hitchman Coal and Coke Company of West Virginia had made its employees promise not to join the United Mine Workers of America.

Justice Brandeis had been introduced to the labor movement many years ago by Mary and Jack O'Sullivan and further shocked into realizing the importance of labor unions by the Pinkerton strikebreakers and by the garment workers' strike. He knew that the union movement was a fact of modern life that the law must recognize and understand.

But after hearing the attorneys argue for both the Hitchman Coal Company and the union officials, a majority of the Supreme Court justices decided that the yellow-dog contract was proper and constitutional. Justice Brandeis could not go along with their decision. Neither could Justices Holmes and

Clarke. Brandeis wrote an eloquent dissenting opinion in which he reviewed the whole history of the case. The mine had been unionized in 1906. When the union closed it with a strike for better working conditions, the company reopened it as a nonunion mine. Thereafter anyone applying for work had to sign a yellow-dog contract. The union was within its right, said Brandeis, Holmes, and Clarke, to want to organize the mine in the first place and represent the workers, and after being shut out, it had a right to persuade the workers to leave their jobs.

The question of the labor unions' right to organize came up again in another way three years later when the Duplex Printing Press Company tried to stop a union from organizing its shop. Again the court upheld the right of the company to exclude the union, and again Justices Brandeis, Holmes, and Clarke disagreed with the court's ruling. Justice Brandeis wrote the dissenting opinion this time, too.

Workers had a right to struggle for a shorter work week and a minimum wage scale. Society was growing more and more industrialized. There must be democratic processes in industry to give workers a voice in their own destiny.

In the continuous procession of cases argued before the Supreme Court, Justice Brandeis often stood with the majority. But during his first ten or twelve years on the bench the Supreme Court had been growing more conservative, particularly on questions of civil rights.

A wire-tapping case raised the civil-rights question of privacy. Brandeis and Sam Warren had made legal history back in 1890 with their essay, "The Right to Privacy," the right of a person to be left alone. Now, nearly forty years later, the case of Olmstead and others versus the United States would give Justice Brandeis the opportunity to add to that earlier contribution he and Sam Warren had made.

The Olmstead case occurred during the days of prohibition and bootlegging. With the help of an expert lineman, federal officers tapped eight phones in the homes and offices of men who were making and selling illegal whiskey. The information they heard secretly on the phones was used as evidence to convict the men, who appealed the case all the way up to the Supreme Court.

Their attorneys presented several good arguments. The strongest was that wiretapping in effect forced the accused to be a witness against himself. In other words, it violated the Fifth Amendment of the Constitution which says, among other things, that no one "shall be compelled in any criminal case to be a witness against himself." Another argument was that it also violated the Fourth Amendment which says, "The right of the people to be secure in their persons, houses, papers, and effects, against un-reasonable searches and seizures, shall not be vio-lated. . . ." The evidence in this case had been se-cured by trickery and trespass.

Yet the Supreme Court upheld the conviction, declaring that the Fourth and Fifth Amendments did not apply. Chief Justice Taft wrote the opinion for the court's majority.

To Louis Brandeis wiretapping was a gross in-vasion of privacy, a form of tyranny. He had to dis-sent once more. If wiretapping were allowed, then as technology advanced "subtler and more far-reach-ing means of invading privacy" would develop. Far-sighted prophecy! In the future, electronic devices would be able to listen through walls, and "bugs" would broadcast every detail of what went on in a person's home.

"Experience should teach us," wrote Justice Brandeis, "to be most on our guard to protect liberty when the government's purposes are beneficent. Men born to freedom are naturally alert to repel in-vasion of their liberty by evil-minded rulers. The greatest dangers to liberty lurk in insidious en-croachment by men of zeal, well-meaning, but with-out understanding. . . . Decency, security and lib-erty alike demand that government officials shall be subjected to the same rules of conduct that are com-mands to the citizen."

Justice Holmes wrote his own dissenting opinion, keeping it short because "brother Brandeis" had stated the case so well. Justices Pierce Butler and Harlan Fiske Stone, both fairly recent appointees, wrote short dissenting statements. Clarke had resigned from the bench, otherwise his opinion might have tipped the scales the other way.

Brandeis's eloquent dissent, added to the influence of his original essay, "The Right to Privacy," helped to change the thinking of lawyers, justices, and lawmakers during the years that followed.

When the Supreme Court closed for the summer of 1920, Justice and Mrs. Brandeis and their daughter Elizabeth sailed for London. With them went Jacob de Haas and Mr. and Mrs. Felix Frankfurter. The voyage was a happy, relaxed time for all of them.

Once again Louis Brandeis was a man bent on a mission, a compelling mission: the first international congress of Zionists since 1913. He knew the situation would be tight with tensions. For one thing, the differences between himself and Chaim Weizmann had been deepening. Since both men were popular and had big followings, an outright break between them would be bad for the whole Zionist movement. Brandeis had no stomach for personal feuds.

When his wife or daughter saw him standing at

the ship's rail, looking out over the sparkling blue surface of the ocean, lost in thought, they knew what troubled him. When they reached their hotel rooms in London and he left them almost at once, they knew where he had gone—to those sessions of the London conference.

Justice Brandeis addressed the opening meeting of the conference on July 7, 1920, in his usual brief and direct way:

> *The effort to acquire the public recognition of the Jewish homeland in Palestine . . . has been crowned with success. The nations of the world have made that recognition. They have done all that they could do. The rest lies with us. The task before us is the Jewish settlement of Palestine. It is the task of reconstruction. We must approve the plans on which the reconstruction shall proceed. We must create the executive and administrative machinery adapted to the work before us. We must select men of the training, the experience and the character fitted to conduct that work. And finally we must devise ways and means to raise the huge sums which the undertaking demands. . . .*

Here, after twenty centuries of suffering, the dream was at last realized! This was what he was trying to tell them. They must not do a mean thing, not now or ever, that would jeopardize their dream-into-reality.

But in the days that followed there was a deepening difference of opinion on how to proceed. Both Brandeis and Weizmann had come armed with plans and ideas for the mandated Palestine, but their plans and ideas were not the same. Brandeis felt that the physical rebuilding of Palestine must come first and that political Zionism could wait. He wanted to get the country on its economic and cultural feet first. Then, some later year, they could press for national independence and an end to Britain's protectorate.

Something else bothered him. During the war years American Jews had carried the responsibility for the movement, and most of the funds donated to the cause of Zionism were American in origin. He wanted American Zionists to have a voice in how those funds were handled.

Chaim Weizmann and his following wanted political Zionism now, that is, they wanted Palestine to become an independent nation; and they wanted control of the world movement back in their own hands. Weizmann was under pressures of intense anti-Semitism that Brandeis had never lived with and could not truly feel. Felix Frankfurter called them "pressures of the whole background of the Russian Pale." Weizmann had seen at close hand the sufferings and persecutions of the Jews of Eastern Europe, and it drove him with a special urgency. He could not think in Brandeis's long-term, objective way.

Needing an ally in America to win the support of the Zionist Organization of America away from Brandeis, Weizmann turned first to Felix Frankfurter. He even asked Frankfurter to move to Palestine.

"Weizmann knew I was a Brandeis man," Mr. Frankfurter wrote about it later, "and he couldn't indulge in open warfare against Brandeis."

But Weizmann did. He found the support he needed in Louis Lipsky of Rochester, New York. Lipsky was an outstanding journalist and Zionist, scholarly, with a long lean face and a firm mouth. He had been active in the movement most of his life and had been present at the emergency session back in 1914 which had elected Louis Brandeis as its chairman.

Lipsky was also a clever politician, for it took him less than a year to oust Brandeis and seize the leadership of the American organization for himself. At the annual congress in Cleveland, Ohio, in 1921, the ZOA was torn with controversy, real and contrived. Heated debates went on for hours over a series of issues, but underneath, it was really a power struggle. Weizmann attended in person to lend the

weight of his influence. When the convention voted
153 to 71 to support the followers of Chaim Weizmann, Louis Brandeis and those who stood with him
handed in their resignations from whatever offices
they held.

A few days later they met in New York City—
about thirty of them—and agreed to continue their
membership in ZOA and to go on working for Palestine. They did not want to damage the greater good
by seceding or forming a minority group within the
movement. Zionism was greater than any of them,
far greater and far more important certainly than
the clash of personalities they had just witnessed.

His repudiation by the Zionists must have hurt
Louis Brandeis very deeply. He had not deserved it
after the contribution he had made with his leadership for so many years. But whatever hurt he felt
disappeared behind his calm. He joined his family at
the shore, to stride along deserted beaches and
breathe deeply of the purifying sea air.

When he returned to Washington in the fall,
the situation in the Supreme Court would be different, possibly even unpleasant. Chief Justice White had
died in the spring, and President Warren G. Harding had appointed William Howard Taft in his
place. Taft had nursed an old resentment against
Brandeis for the embarrassment of the Ballinger in-
quiry during his Presidency. In 1916 Taft had bit-

terly opposed Brandeis's appointment to the bench.

He and Brandeis had not met until two years afterward, when they accidentally passed each other one day on the street. Taft had stopped, turned, and asked, "Isn't this Justice Brandeis? I don't think we have ever met."

"We met at Harvard," Brandeis reminded him, "after your return from the Philippines." (Taft had headed the Philippine commission after the United States acquired the islands from Spain.) Since they were in front of Brandeis's apartment house, Justice Brandeis invited him in. Taft accepted, and they talked for half an hour, discovering that they did share points of agreement.

That had been in 1918. Now in 1921 they would begin working together, and the association would last eight years. Taft proved that he was not a petty man. He could rise above his own feelings, particularly now that he had gained the position on the court he had coveted so long.

President Harding had the opportunity to make three more appointments to the Supreme Court. George Sutherland replaced Clarke. The other two were Pierce Butler of Minnesota and Edward Terry Sanford of Tennessee. That much of a turnover was bound to make a difference in the viewpoint of the court. There would be times in the future when Holmes and Brandeis would stand together against the other justices: "Holmes and Brandeis dissenting."

The conservative quality of the court was never more apparent than in 1923 when it heard the case of *Adkins et al.* v. *the Children's Hospital of the District of Columbia.* "*Adkins et al.*" was the Minimum Wage Board of the District, which was trying to protect women working in hospitals and hotels from substandard pay.

The lawyers for the wage board argued that there had been unfair depression of wages for women workers, that their pay was so low they could not live on it and keep their health. Attorneys for the employers argued that a minimum wage law was unconstitutional, that it was a price-fixing law, interfering with freedom of contract between employer and employee.

The court decided in favor of the employer. It declared the minimum wage law of the District of Columbia unconstitutional. Even Chief Justice Taft considered the decision unwise and dissented, as did Justices Sanford and Holmes. Justice Brandeis was deeply pleased with Taft's dissent, but he himself had not sat on the case, perhaps because of the fact that he had argued for the Oregon minimum wage law before the Supreme Court and because his own daughter was secretary of the board at the time.

The Supreme Court decision ended the board and Elizabeth's job. She decided to continue her studies in law and economics at the University of Wisconsin in Madison, where John R. Commons was teaching and building an exceptionally fine department. She remained to take her Ph.D. and to meet and marry Paul Raushenbush, who had gone to Madison to work with Dr. Commons.

Paul Raushenbush eventually became director of the Unemployment Compensation Department of the Wisconsin Industrial Commission. He and Elizabeth both taught economics at the university in the 1920's. When Dr. Commons wrote his four-volume *History of Labor in the United States,* Elizabeth Brandeis wrote the whole section in the third volume on labor legislation.

Justice Brandeis had been through some very dark hours, but there were as many light, even bright to dazzling. Both of his daughters were scholarly, low-voiced gentlewomen, devoted to him and to Alice. Elizabeth's particular concern for labor problems was profoundly gratifying.

Susan was a practicing attorney in New York City handling a variety of legal matters. During the 1920's she argued a case before the United States Supreme Court, and her father naturally excused himself from participation in that instance. Susan also worked for the federal government for several years on major antitrust cases. The deeper she went into law, the easier she found it to communicate with her father. Now he exchanged almost daily notes, messages, and letters with her as he did with his brother Alfred.

In 1925 Susan Brandeis married Jacob H. Gilbert whom she had first met as an opposing attorney in a lawsuit. They practiced law together. Susan followed her father's example and became a leader in the national women's Zionist organization, Hadassah. Later she served for thirteen years on the New York State Board of Regents which supervises public education in that state.

With both daughters gone from the household except for occasional visits, Louis and Alice Brandeis were bound to feel a little desolate until they became accustomed to their new situation. But they both lived such full and useful lives, and were blessed with so much self-reliance that their adjustment was scarcely noticeable to others. In 1926 they moved to another Washington apartment house, Florence Court on California Street. There the justice's office was a small room off the main hall of the apartment, containing a desk, a chair, and a couch. On the floor above he had another small apartment. His secretary worked in one room, and in the other he kept most of his files and books.

Justice and Mrs. Brandeis had begun in 1924 to

make great, long-term plans for the University of Louisville. Kentucky would always be a kind of returning point for Justice Brandeis—the scene of his birth, boyhood years, and early schooling, the region where he had learned to cherish individual freedom, where many of his family still lived. He had gone home very recently for a long visit with Alfred at Ladless Hill Farm on Upper River Road. (Alfred called his farm "Ladless" because he had four daughters and no sons.) The two aging brothers sat in the Kentucky sunshine and talked for hours about their families, their children, their friends, and their lives, as well as the future of the university. Louis wanted Alfred to take charge of the family's assistance to the university, with help from other members of the family.

"To become great, a university must express the people whom it serves and must express the people and community at their best" was the way Justice Brandeis explained his views. He particularly wanted the university to be Kentuckian, with every kind of Kentucky history and biography in its libraries. He intended to donate his own collections of books, papers, and little-known pamphlets. The law school especially must become one of the finest in the country. With increased endowment and improved teaching staff, the University of Louisville flowered into a dynamic center of learning. After

Alfred's death in 1928 at the age of seventy-four, the justice continued his interest in the university under its president, Dr. Raymond A. Kent.

Louis Brandeis was destined to become a leading influence in the Zionist movement once more. The old wound that the Zionists had dealt him, probably a deeper hurt than he ever admitted to anyone, had been healing steadily. More and more Zionists were coming to realize what a mistake they had made to change leadership. Without his inspirational appeal, the whole movement in America had been slowing down, membership in the Zionist Organization of America falling off. There were deep cleavage lines within the group, and the disunity existed during the same years that the situation in Palestine was going from bad to worse.

The first British high commissioner of Palestine was Sir Herbert Samuel. Among his first problems was Arab opposition to the idea of a national Jewish homeland. In spite of the fact that he was himself Jewish and a Zionist, some of Samuel's decisions showed a lack of understanding of the deep feelings of both Jews and Arabs. Riots broke out; Jewish colonies were attacked. The worst outbreak occurred in 1929 when whole Jewish communities were massacred.

Such a powder-keg situation could involve all the major powers. Justice Brandeis knew this, and he was not surprised to receive an invitation in November 1929 to address an emergency meeting in Washington of worried businessmen and other concerned persons. Because of his position on the Supreme Court bench he usually remained aloof from political activity, but he did consent to participate this time.

"The road to a Jewish Palestine is economic, and the opportunity is open," he told the meeting. "I reached this conviction ten years ago when I became acquainted on my visit there with the country and the people, both Arabs and Jews."

The climate of Palestine is a lot like southern California; it needed irrigation. Jewish pioneers had already proved that it could be made into a land flowing with milk and honey. "Touched by intelligent effort supplemented by science, it began to bloom almost as a miracle." Palestine needed money to carry on that development, and Brandeis cautioned that all plans for Palestine must take into account the best interest of all the inhabitants there: Moslem and Christian as well as Jew.

He had expressed his confidence in Britain's administration of Palestine and felt it would "discharge fully the obligation assumed." But Britain was losing her enthusiasm for the spirit of the Balfour Declaration. The following spring a commission issued an official report on the 1929 riots, showing frank sympathy for the Arab cause. It went further and recommended that Jewish immigration into Palestine be reduced.

That was shocking. Brandeis felt, and said, that American Zionists must protest this. Many agreed with him, but now when Palestine needed their help the most, they were too divided among themselves to be effective.

Then the hour had come to reunite. Some called Louis Lipsky's presidency a "petty and punitive oligarchy." Said others, "The ZOA is morally and politically bankrupt." The whole situation came to a head at the thirty-third annual convention in Cleveland in July 1930.

When President Lipsky addressed the meeting, the audience was hostile. At a banquet on Sunday to raise money for the ZOA almost no funds were forthcoming. Lipsky had to yield to the mood of the conference. He called a temporary adjournment. All day Monday there were small meetings, rumors, lobbying, phone calls to New York and Boston.

At eleven o'clock that night President Lipsky went before the entire convention to read a letter from Louis Brandeis in which the justice agreed to give his active support to a reunited Zionist Organization of America. Everyone was too tired that night to celebrate the victory, but next day the cheers went up when Jacob de Haas came to the platform and shook hands with Louis Lipsky.

In Washington, D. C., the seventy-four-year-old justice began at once to use his influence in both England and America to work out a solution of the Arab-Jewish conflict in Palestine.

The United States was emerging into her own new kind of unity and away from disharmony and reaction. In the 1932 Presidential election Franklin Delano Roosevelt received a mandate from the American people to look forward and move ahead with the kind of social legislation that Louis Brandeis had always wanted.

Chapter 13

HE NEVER LOST INTEREST

*"We must be ever on our guard, lest
we erect our prejudices into legal
principles. If we would guide by
the light of reason, we must let our
minds be bold."*

Justice Brandeis watched from his position on the Supreme Court as the destiny of his country unfolded. He watched, gave sound advice to those willing to listen, made predictions that came true. As far back as 1923 he had predicted in one of his legal opinions that the economy would collapse unless inflation and speculation were curbed. He had warned a public utility company then against demanding higher and higher rates. Everyone was greedily pressing for more—more wages, more income, higher prices, greater profits. Even when danger signs began to appear—a serious pinch for the cotton growers in the South, increasing unemployment in New England—the pressures upward into the inflation spiral continued. Finally the bubble broke; the stock market collapsed in October 1929; and utility rates, wages, prices, profits, all came sliding down. Unemployment increased until there were millions of idle people, many of them literally starving.

When Franklin Delano Roosevelt was elected President in 1932, the United States was at the bottom of the deepest depression in its history. But the complete change of party—Democratic President, Democratic Congress—and the vigorous way in which FDR plunged in at once to draft new laws to help cure the depression, created excitement and hope. It was to be a New Deal for the American people.

Brandeis was deeply gratified to know that the new President was consulting such men as Felix Frankfurter in selecting people to fill posts in the new administration. He and Alice had been friends for so many years with the Frankfurters that they felt very much in tune with the new, courageous trends.

"Will you take a position in the government yourself?" they asked Professor Frankfurter.

No, he told them. He knew the President wanted him as Solicitor General, but he felt he could be more useful as a behind-the-scenes adviser, much as Brandeis had been for Wilson.

Many of the men whom President Roosevelt appointed were frankly disciples of Justice Brandeis. FDR had admired Brandeis for a long time, and would soon be calling him Isaiah.

Justice Brandeis watched the Congress and the President pass fifteen new and sometimes radical laws during the first hundred days they were in office. Some made him deeply happy. Others he felt had not been thought through carefully enough. The Brandeis teas took on a new excitement as guests rushed to them, eager to talk of their work in fighting the depression. The justice, however, could express no opinions on the new laws, because later on he might be ruling on cases involving their constitutionality.

One of the earliest of the new laws created the CCC—the Civilian Conservation Corps. It was a program to gather up despairing, destitute young men in city street gangs or living like hobos along the railroad tracks and put them to work in the fresh air, refurbishing parks, planting trees in dust bowl areas. Some were so young they had never had a chance to start working. "Men are not bad, men are not degraded, because they desire to be so," Brandeis had once said of Boston's paupers. It is the "main duty of those who are dealing with these unfortunates to help them up and let them feel in one way or another that there is some hope for them in life."

Soon the President signed into law the Federal Emergency Relief Act to rush money to the states to feed the starving. The Emergency Farm Mortgage Act and the Home Owners' Loan Act loaned money to people so that they would not lose their farms and homes. When a man could not sell his crops or find work, he had no money to meet the monthly payments on his mortgage. Whoever had loaned him the mortgage on his premises, usually a bank, would then foreclose and take the place away from him. Government loans helped to prevent such tragedies. And the AAA—Agricultural Adjustment Act—made possible nationwide soil conservation and planning of crops.

The TVA—Tennessee Valley Authority—was one of the most amazing accomplishments of that first hundred days, and it kicked up a storm of debate. The TVA was authorized by Congress to build a system of dams along the Tennessee River to create water power. In one of the most poverty-stricken regions in the country, TVA would mean flood control, cheap electricity, reforestation, redeemed farmland, low-cost housing, new local industries, and employment. Senator George W. Norris of Nebraska, who had worked and pleaded for such a project for years, saw his dream come true in a program that went far beyond his own original expectations. He called it "the most wonderful and far-reaching humanitarian document that has ever come from the White House." Justice Brandeis thought so, too. "I like the sample," said Brandeis to Senator Norris. "I'd like to order half a dozen."

But NRA—National Industrial Recovery Act—was one of the new laws that showed lack of clear thinking. The administration had apparently grown heady on its own power, and the minority in Congress wasn't strong enough to stop it. NRA was a big, clumsy law that included almost everything. Through the cooperation of industry it was going to provide shorter hours, higher wages, fair-trade practice, collective bargaining between management and labor, not to mention projects to create jobs, such as constructing roads and public buildings. It attempted to do so many things at once that its director found the act almost impossible to enforce.

After those first hundred days the headiness began to wear off, the minority in Congress to grow more vigorous. Justice Brandeis felt relieved to see the first quick-money—"pump-priming"—policies subside. Soon the New Deal seemed to mature into a more responsible and thoughtful approach, writing carefully planned laws for long term social reform.

The Securities Act of 1933 and the Banking Act of the same year could have come from Justice Brandeis's own pen. The Securities Act regulated the purchase and sale of stocks and bonds to protect the investor from fraud. Any company issuing stock had to publish a complete set of accurate facts and figures about the condition of the company. Something the New Haven had had to learn the hard way.

As for the Banking Act—well, twenty years ago Justice Brandeis had written a book called *Other People's Money—and How the Bankers Use It*. It had first been a series of articles in *Harper's Weekly*, when Norman Hapgood was editor of the magazine. In it Brandeis spoke gravely of that worst monopoly of all—money. Investment bankers like J. P. Morgan when they combined their resources could control the whole economy by controlling railroads, public services, insurance companies, and industry. Sometimes they had interlocking directorates, that is, the same men would be officers in several companies. There must be laws to prevent these powerful combines, to emancipate business and restore industrial liberty. He went on in his book to develop his ideas on what these laws should be.

The book had attracted little attention at the time, but suddenly in the 1930's it became a best seller. New Dealers turned to it for ideas and quoted it right and left to explain what they were doing.

The Banking Act of 1933 created insurance on bank deposits. That is, it created the Federal Bank Deposit Insurance Corporation, a special insurance company, to guarantee depositors against loss up to five thousand dollars. Later the amount was increased. This helped the smallest depositors most of all; those who saved their money a little bit at a time could be sure they would not lose their savings if the bank failed. After the crash in 1929, banks had failed all over the country, had simply closed their doors never to open them again. People who had their money in them lost everything. This new law would prevent such a thing from happening again.

The Banking Act also went after money monopolies by stating that anyone in the commercial banking business could not also be in the investment banking business. J. P. Morgan and his associates,

for instance, were known to control thirty-four
banks and all the money deposited in them. He also
controlled many other companies through his huge
investments. Under this new law, he could no longer
be the banker of the companies he controlled or
speculate with other people's money.

"The banker should be detached from the business for which he performs the banking service,"
Justice Brandeis had said in *Harper's Weekly* twenty
years before. No wonder FDR compared him to the
prophet Isaiah.

As Louis Dembitz Brandeis approached his
eightieth birthday, hair snow white, tall slender
figure just slightly bent, he was still looking ahead.
He looked ahead to the end of another poor man's
problem: irregularity of employment. In spite of the
jobs created by the New Deal there were still millions out of work, and the problem troubled him
more than ever. Far too many of the unemployed
were poor the minute their jobs stopped, because
they had no savings; they had no savings because
their jobs were seasonal and they had to spread their
earnings over the whole year. What good was it for
a man to make a high wage if he earned it only part
of the year and earned nothing the rest?

"My thought is to do away with day-labor . . .
by declaring the right to continuity of employment."

The right to work all year round? Yes. He believed that unions should add that right to the other demands they were making:

> *The right to regularity of employment is co-equal with the right to regularity in the payment of rent, in the payment of interest on bonds. . . . No business is successfully conducted which does not perform fully the obligations incident to each of these rights. No dividend should be paid until each of these charges has been met. The reserve to insure regularity of employment is as imperative as the reserve for depreciation. . . . No business is socially solvent without it.*

There was another way to attack irregular employment. It was all the more apparent and urgent in the bottom of a depression: unemployment compensation, a kind of insurance that would continue a worker on pay or part-pay for several weeks after his job had ended. It could sustain him and his family while he searched for another job.

Justice Brandeis had lived with the problem for years and had discussed it with leading people—at dinner parties or the famous teas in his home—and most important of all with his two gifted daughters.

Back in 1921 Dr. John R. Commons had drafted

one of the first state laws on the subject. Year after year liberals in the Wisconsin legislature had tried to get the bill passed. But jobs were plentiful in those years, and no one worried about unemployment too much. At last in 1932, the worst year of the depression, the Wisconsin legislature enacted the Wisconsin Unemployment Compensation Act. It was called the "Wisconsin Plan," providing that employers pay into a state reserve fund a certain amount of payroll tax. The money in the fund would be used to sustain the unemployed.

Of course, Elizabeth and Paul Raushenbush were deeply involved. Mr. Raushenbush became director of Wisconsin's Unemployment Compensation Department. They corresponded constantly with Justice Brandeis about it, told him about Wisconsin's progress whenever they came east on a visit to Washington or Cape Cod.

There was always more time at Cape Cod for all of them to relax and converse—around the dinner table or on the wooden rocking chairs and benches on the front porch.

Now when Elizabeth or Susan came to visit the aging justice at Cape Cod, they brought his grandchildren. Louis Gilbert was the oldest—almost eleven. After him came Alice Gilbert and Walter Raushenbush. Frank Gilbert was the youngest. Alice was one of his favorites, perhaps because she was the only girl of the four. He would pick her up in his arms and say, "Come see Alice. Come see Alice in her new blue dress."

The four of them often trailed along with him on adventuresome walks, collecting treasures in the bags he had remembered to bring. As he grew older, the walks had to be shorter. In his last years his grandchildren used to make "appointments" to see him in his study and talk with him. He liked to draw his grandchildren and his nieces and nephews into serious talks. To one he said, "Never mistake a mind for a memory. I have both." Walter was amazed to learn from him that you could live on a piece of land without paying rent *if you owned it.* "I pay rent on the apartment in Washington," Grandfather Brandeis explained. "But I *own* the house in Cape Cod."

They were always as hungry as he had been at that age. But at the dinner table Grandmother Brandeis—who still did the carving and serving— frowned if they wanted more than second and third helpings.

"Oh, Grandmother," said Walter one day. "You're tight."

She had been so frugal all of her life, she could not change.

Neither could her husband stop thinking of social problems all during the summer at Cape Cod.

Unemployment lived with him, and he lived

with it. Other states were considering the Wisconsin Plan, but they were moving too slowly. The real solution should be a federal law, which would give states an incentive to follow Wisconsin.

Then something began to happen which he was grateful he had lived long enough to see. The New Deal administration was designing a social security law to provide pensions for the aged. There was every reason in the world why that law should include a provision for unemployment insurance.

Men in high places had learned long ago to listen to his advice. They listened this time, too, to the prophet Isaiah as President Roosevelt called him. Concerned businessmen, such as Lincoln Filene and others, came to the Brandeises' apartment to ask him how federal action could induce the states to pass unemployment insurance laws. The justice suggested a "tax offset device," that is, a federal tax on employers which they would not have to pay if their state passed a proper unemployment compensation law supported by a payroll tax. This would speed state action. A second Brandeis, his daughter Elizabeth, and her husband, Paul Raushenbush, had a hand in turning the unemployment compensation suggestion into a bill. It was first introduced in Congress in 1934 and became part of the Social Security Act that passed the following year.

It was another of his extraordinary contributions to a better life in America—a better life through better laws. Yet Louis Brandeis's greatest role was as an associate justice of the United States Supreme Court. By the time FDR was elected to the Presidency, Louis D. Brandeis had been on the bench sixteen years, his influence deepening with each session. He was no longer ninth in the procession of justices who filed from their chambers into the courtroom, but third behind the chief justice, now Charles Evans Hughes. Only two men had been on the bench longer: Willis Van Devanter of Wyoming and James Clark McReynolds of Tennessee. Brandeis moved among all of them as a respected jurist, one who himself felt a deep, almost reverential respect for the dignity of the Supreme Court and its procedures.

Now in all its dignity and solemn responsibility the Supreme Court was to weigh and evaluate the laws passed by the New Deal administration, as one after another would be argued before it in a test case. Only two other justices were as consistently liberal in their thinking as Brandeis. One was Harlan Fiske Stone, appointed long ago by President Coolidge; the other was Benjamin Nathan Cardozo, appointed by President Hoover in 1932 when Justice Oliver Wendell Holmes retired.

Because the whole New Deal was so experimental, it was debated violently most of the time. Those

who opposed it did so because they feared that too
much power in the national government was dangerous or that too much of its planning was undemocratic. And there was growing opposition from Republicans as the party out of power. For those who
wanted to bring the New Deal under control the
only realistic way to fight it was through the courts.

The first law up for examination was NRA—the
cumbersome package that tried to gallop in so many
directions at once. A poultry company had been
convicted in a lower court for violating a regulation
of NRA. It became the test case; the attorneys for
the company arguing that NRA was unconstitutional
because it delegated too much power to one man,
the President, giving him a kind of one-man economic rule over too many areas of business. This
time the court decided unanimously that NRA *was*
unconstitutional. It did give too much authority to
one man, and Congress had no right to do so. It was
"big government" in spirit, and Justice Brandeis for
one considered that just as much of a curse as bigness in business if it got out of hand.

When another test case brought the Agricultural Adjustment Act before the Supreme Court, the
decision was not unanimous. A majority of the justices declared it unconstitutional on the grounds
that Congress had again gone beyond its proper
bounds in granting too much authority to the bu-

reau which ran the AAA. Justices Brandeis, Cardozo, and Stone dissented. To them it was entirely proper that the federal government seek to regulate agriculture.

TVA had stirred up so much controversy that it was bound to provoke a test case. Its power plant was generating cheap electricity for the region, among other things, and the loud complaint was that it was competing with private enterprise. A group of stockholders had brought the action to stop the directors of their electric power company, The Alabama Power Company, from selling their transmission lines and property to the government, to connect them in a system with the government's power plant. The Alabama Power could not do business with the TVA, their counsel argued, because the TVA had no right to exist. The TVA Act of 1933 was unconstitutional.

All nine men on the bench, who listened to the oral argument and studied the written briefs of both sides, were in their posts because they had free and independent minds. Their positions were for life, so that they could make sound decisions free of political pressure. This time all but one conservative stood with Justices Brandeis, Stone, and Cardozo in upholding TVA. In a concurring opinion, Justice Brandeis raised important procedural issues about the right of the plaintiffs to bring this lawsuit. He was always concerned about the maintenance of proper standards of judicial review.

The Supreme Court and the United States had the benefit of Louis D. Brandeis's talents for another four years, until 1939. His opinions were often predictable, especially when he supported laws limiting working hours and setting minimum wages.

But his energies were running out, and he knew it. Alice supervised him carefully so that he would not overexert himself. He must save his best for the court. She still held teas, but they were small, and the justice remained in his chair as guest after guest came forward to pay respects to the venerable gentleman who seemed to look more fragile with each passing day. There was plenty of fire in his mind, and it showed in his sparkling eyes whenever anyone said something to challenge or amuse him. He spent his summers at Chatham as he had done for years.

In spite of his care, he was ill during the winter of 1938–1939. It alarmed his family and friends. But after a month he felt well enough to return to the court and take up his duties once more. Alice had to allow it.

At the end of one week Justice Brandeis knew what he knew, and on February 13, 1939, he sent in his resignation to the President.

"My dear Mr. Justice Brandeis," the President

replied. "There is nothing I can do but to accede to your retirement. But with this goes the knowledge that our long association will continue, and the hope that you will be spared for many long years to come to render additional services to mankind."

"I am not retiring because of ill health," the eighty-two-year-old justice assured his family in out-of-the-way places like Kentucky.

From faraway Madison, Wisconsin, Elizabeth wrote to him at once.

> *2228 Hillington Green*
> *Madison, Wisconsin*
> *February 14, 1939*

> *Dearest Father:—*
>   *It is hard for me to write. All the things I want to say sound mawkish—or presumptuous from me to you. I cannot bear to use any words at this time that do not ring true. I hope you know what is in my heart even if I cannot get it said.*
>   *I know that there is no cause for grieving. Everything must have an end. And the life and work that you can look back upon must give you contentment and satisfaction. As for me, my appreciation of what you are and have done*

*keeps increasing as I grow older and better able
to understand.*

*If the lessons you have taught do not seem
to have been learned very well yet, that is not
for any lack on your part. Measuring my words,
I do not see how any one person could have
done more than you have done.*

*But of course I do feel sad—regardless. I
suppose ends are always sad. Paul and I, along
with hundreds, probably thousands, of others,
will be trying to carry on different parts of your
work and trying to catch something of the spirit
in which you have worked. But we shall all
know how inadequate we are and how far we
fall short of the standards you set. But I know
you will be generous in your judgment of us,
and at least, despite our other limitations, our
love and our admiration for you will continue to
be just about unlimited!*

Elizabeth

Justice and Mrs. Brandeis continued to spend
their winters in Washington, D.C.

People still sought his advice, patiently accepting Alice's limitation on the length of their visits.
Young people who wanted guidance in planning
their careers sometimes came away startled by what

he told them, even a little angry, until they had lived with his suggestion a while.

More than one saw bigger opportunities in the national capital than in their home towns. To each he would say, "Take your training and talents back to the service of your own community, your hinterland, and lead a full life there."

"But Mr. Justice—Fargo, North Dakota!" cried one.

The justice believed that you began all the way back at the beginning, in the village and town and their unpaid opportunities to hold public office, to build a sound democracy.

When a reporter in Oregon, eager to be a high-powered news correspondent, wrote to Justice Brandeis about it, the justice replied cordially,

"Stay in Oregon."

To the end of his days Louis Dembitz Brandeis never lost interest in the progress of any of his hopes and projects: savings-bank life insurance, year-round employment, regulation of monopolies, Zionism, the labor movement, and all the important social reforms happening around him. After his retirement he watched the news carefully and kept in touch with younger men carrying out his ideas.

News from abroad had been alarming for a long time. Hitler had risen to power in Germany and had begun at once to build a war machine, reoccupying regions that Germany had lost in World War I. Within Germany the rise of Hitler's Nazi party meant the brutal persecution of Jews there.

By the time Justice Brandeis retired from the Supreme Court, Europe was teetering on the brink of another world war, and the British government was struggling to forestall it. In the spring of that year Britain issued the famous—or infamous—White Paper on Palestine, which repudiated the Balfour Declaration and set a severe limitation on Jewish immigration into Palestine.

"What does the world propose to do with the Jews for whom exile is enforced?" Justice Brandeis wrote to the president of the Zionist Organization of America.

Europe plunged into World War II before the end of the year, and the change to Prime Minister Churchill's administration meant that the creation of a Jewish nation, one day to be called Israel, would have to wait until the war was over.

A bout of pneumonia left Justice Brandeis rather frail in 1940, and a heart condition prevented him from climbing stairs. He lived on the first floor at Chatham. Alice seldom left his side, caring for him, reading to him when he wished, helping him to make the most of the strength he still had.

"I could not have lived my life without Alice,"

he said, knowing full well that his course was almost run.

The course had been a splendid one, and it continued in his will. He established trust funds to support his wife and each of his daughters so that they could live free lives. The rest of his three-million-dollar estate went to the University of Louisville, Zionism, and a group working for civil liberties and workers' education. During the past thirty-five years his donations had been tremendous. He had already given more than half a million dollars to Zionism and Jewish charities, two hundred thousand to the continuing campaign for savings-bank life insurance, and similar amounts to education and needy individuals.

The news from abroad continued to sadden him, but he never knew about Pearl Harbor.

On the thirtieth of September, 1941, a heart attack brought the doctor hurrying to his bedside in the Washington apartment. His strength ebbed away steadily during the next few days until he lost consciousness, and on Sunday, October fifth, he was gone. His ashes were taken home to Louisville, to be placed under the walk before the entrance to the University of Louisville Law School. Alice's were placed beside his four years later.

Tributes to the great jurist poured out of people the world around. "The law of truth was in his mouth," said Justice Frankfurter, quoting from the Old Testament. Speaking at his funeral service, Dean Acheson said, "Whatever dark days may lie ahead, the memory of the Justice will be a voice always saying to us, 'Lift up your hearts!'"

Paul A. Freund, who had come to Washington from the Harvard Law School to be Justice Brandeis's law clerk and returned to a full professorship at Harvard, called him "the most powerful moral teacher ever to have sat on our highest court."

Epilogue

"His whole life was devoted to keeping the shackles off people. He insisted that each individual was entitled to room to grow to the full stature of his own personality. He fought bigness in the cloak of monopoly all his life because he believed that monopoly impoverished human personality. That belief was not merely for contemplation: it was a fighting faith.

"Most of his life was cast in the role of a non-conformist to the conventional views of the day, but there was nothing negative in his make-up. Every disagreement carried with it a solution. He premised everything on facts, in the assembly of which he had no equal.

"He did as much to change the thought of the nation and the outlook of his government concerning American life as any person of his time. Fortunately he lived to see his philosophy become that of his government. He proved not only the right to dissent in America but also that dissent can be constructive."

—Chief Justice Earl Warren,
speaking at Brandeis University,
November 11, 1956.

Suggested Further
Reading

Acheson, Dean. *Morning and Noon*. Boston: Houghton Mifflin Company, 1965.

Blumberg, Dorothy Rose. *Florence Kelley, The Making of a Social Pioneer*. New York: Augustus M. Kelley, 1966.

De Haas, Jacob. *Louis D. Brandeis*. New York: Bloch Publishing Company, 1929.

Filene, A. Lincoln. *A Merchant's Horizon*. Boston: Houghton Mifflin Company, 1924.

Frankfurter, Felix. *Felix Frankfurter Reminisces: Recorded Talks with Dr. Harlan B. Phillips*. New York: Reynal & Company, 1960.

Freund, Paul A. *The Supreme Court of the United States*. Cleveland: The World Publishing Company, 1961.

Hapgood, Norman. *The Changing Years*. New York: Farrar & Rinehart, Inc., 1930.

Johnson, Alvin. *Pioneer's Progress*. New York: The Viking Press, 1952.

Lief, Alfred. *Brandeis, The Personal History of an American Ideal*. New York: Stackpole Sons, 1936.

Mason, Alpheus Thomas. *Brandeis, A Free Man's Life*. New York: The Viking Press, 1946.

Payne, Robert. *The Splendor of Israel*. New York: Harper & Row, Publishers, 1963.

Staples, Henry Lee, and Mason, Alpheus Thomas. *The Fall of a Railroad Empire*. Syracuse: Syracuse University Press, 1947.

Todd, A. L. *Justice on Trial, The Case of Louis D. Brandeis*. New York: McGraw-Hill Book Company, 1964.

Weizmann, Chaim. *Trial and Error*. New York: Harper & Brothers, 1949.

Bibliography

BOOKS

Abrams, Richard M. *Conservatism in a Progressive Era.* Cambridge: Harvard University Press, 1964.

Acheson, Dean. *Morning and Noon.* Boston: Houghton Mifflin Company, 1965.

Baedeker, Karl. *Palestine and Syria.* Leipzig: Karl Baedeker, Publisher, 1906.

Berman, Edward. *Life Insurance, A Critical Examination.* New York: Harper & Brothers, Publishers, 1936.

Bickel, Alexander M. *The Unpublished Opinions of Mr. Justice Brandeis.* Cambridge: The Belknap Press, 1957.

Blumberg, Dorothy Rose. *Florence Kelley, The Making of a Social Pioneer.* New York: Augustus M. Kelley, 1966.

Brandeis, Louis D. *Brandeis On Zionism.* Washington: Zionist Organization of America, 1942.

———. *Business, A Profession.* Boston: Small, Maynard & Company, 1914.

———. *The Curse of Bigness, Miscellaneous Papers.* New York: The Viking Press, 1934.

———. *Other People's Money—and How the Bankers Use It.* New York: Frederick A. Stokes Co., 1914.

Casseday, Ben. *The History of Louisville from Its Earliest Settlement Till the Year 1852.* Louisville: Hull and Brother, 1852.

Cohen, Israel. *The Zionist Movement.* London: Frederick Muller Ltd., 1945.

Commons, John R. *History of Labor in the United States, 1896–1932.* Volume III. Section on "Labor Legislation" written by Elizabeth Brandeis, Ph. D. New York: The Macmillan Company, 1935.

282

De Haas, Jacob. *Louis D. Brandeis.* New York: Block Publishing Company, 1929.

Dilliard, Irving, editor. *Mr. Justice Brandeis, Great American.* St. Louis: The Modern View Press, 1941.

Dry, Camille N. *Pictorial St. Louis, A Topographical Survey 1875.* St. Louis: Compton & Company, 1876.

Dugdale, Blanche E. *Arthur James Balfour.* New York: G. P. Putnam's Sons, 1937.

Filene, A. Lincoln. *A Merchant's Horizon.* Boston: Houghton Mifflin Company, 1924.

Frankfurter, Felix. *Felix Frankfurter Reminisces: Recorded Talks with Dr. Harlan B. Phillips.* New York: Reynal & Company, 1960.

——, Editor. *Mr. Justice Brandeis.* New Haven: Yale University Press, 1932.

Freund, Paul A. *The Supreme Court of the United States.* Cleveland: The World Publishing Company, 1961.

Frischauer, Paul. *The Imperial Crown.* London: Cassell and Company Limited, 1939.

Goldman, Solomon, Editor. *The Words of Justice Brandeis.* New York: Henry Schuman, 1953.

Goldmark, Josephine. *Impatient Crusader.* Urbana: University of Illinois Press, 1953. Preface by Elizabeth Brandeis who completed the manuscript revisions after her aunt's death in December 1950.

——. *Pilgrims of '48.* New Haven: Yale University Press, 1930.

Hannah Winthrop Chapter D. A. R. *Historic Guide to Cambridge.* Cambridge: 1907.

Hapgood, Norman. *The Changing Years.* New York: Farrar & Rinehart, Inc., 1930.

Hofstadter, Samuel H., and Horowitz, George. *The Right of Privacy.* New York: Central Book Company, 1964.

Johnson, Alvin. *Pioneer's Progress*. New York: The Viking Press, 1952.

King, Moses. *King's Handbook of Boston*. Cambridge: Moses King Publisher, 1878.

Klinkhamer, Sister Marie Carolyn. *Edward Douglas White, Chief Justice of the United States*. Washington: The Catholic University of America Press, 1943.

Konefsky, Samuel J. *The Legacy of Holmes and Brandeis*. New York: The Macmillan Company, 1956.

Lansdale, Maria Hornor. *Vienna and the Viennese*. Philadelphia: Henry T. Coates & Co., 1902.

Levensohn, Lotta. *Outline of Zionist History*. New York: Scopus Publishing Company, Inc., 1941.

Lief, Alfred. *Brandeis, The Personal History of an American Ideal*. New York: Stackpole Sons, 1936.

――――. *The Brandeis Guide to the Modern World*. Boston: Little, Brown and Company, 1941.

――――. *The Social and Economic Views of Mr. Justice Brandeis*. New York: The Vanguard Press, 1930.

Lutzow, Count. *The Story of Prague*. London: J. M. Dent & Co., 1902.

McCrackan, W. D. *The New Palestine*. London: Jonathan Cape, 1922.

McDowell, Robert Emmett. *City of Conflict, Louisville in the Civil War 1861–1865*. 1962.

Mann, Arthur. *Yankee Reformers in the Urban Age*. Cambridge: The Belknap Press, 1954; Harper Torchbook, 1966.

Mason, Alpheus Thomas. *Brandeis, A Free Man's Life*. New York: The Viking Press, 1946.

――――. *Brandeis: Lawyer and Judge in the Modern State*. Princeton: Princeton University Press, 1933.

――――. *The Brandeis Way, A Case Study in the Workings of Democracy*. Princeton: Princeton University Press, 1938.

――――. *Bureaucracy Convicts Itself, The Ballinger-Pinchot Controversy of 1910*. New York: The Viking Press, 1941.

――――. *William Howard Taft: Chief Justice*. New York: Simon and Schuster, Inc., 1964.

Merrill, Estelle M. H., Editor. *Cambridge Sketches by Cambridge Authors*. Cambridge: Young Women's Christian Association, 1896.

Messmer, Charles Kanoker. *City in Conflict, A History of Louisville 1860–1865*. Manuscript, Thesis for M. A. at University of Kentucky, Lexington, 1953.

Monroe, Will S. *Bohemia and the Czechs*. Boston: The Page Company, 1910.

Morison, Samuel Eliot. *Three Centuries of Harvard 1636– 1936*. Cambridge: Harvard University Press, 1937.

Payne, Robert. *The Splendor of Israel*. New York: Harper & Row, Publishers, 1963.

Perlman, Selig. *A History of Trade Unionism in the United States*. New York: Augustus M. Kelley, Inc., 1922.

Pollack, Ervin H., Editor. *The Brandeis Reader*. New York: Oceana Publications, 1956.

Rabinowitz, Ezekiel. *Justice Louis D. Brandeis, The Zionist Chapter of His Life*. New York: Philosophical Society, 1968.

Rath, R. John. *The Viennese Revolution of 1848*. Austin: University of Texas Press, 1957.

Shurtleff, Nathaniel B. *A Topographical and Historical Description of Boston*. Boston: Printed by request of the City Council, 1871.

Staples, Henry Lee, and Mason, Alpheus Thomas. *The Fall of a Railroad Empire.* Syracuse: Syracuse University Press, 1947.

Stein, Leonard. *The Balfour Declaration.* New York: Simon and Schuster, Inc., 1961.

Thomas, Helen Shirley. *Felix Frankfurter, Scholar on the Bench.* Baltimore: The Johns Hopkins Press, 1960.

Todd, A. L. *Justice on Trial, The Case of Louis D. Brandeis.* New York: McGraw-Hill Book Company, 1964.

Warren, Charles. *History of the Harvard Law School,* Volume II. New York: Lewis Publishing Company, 1908.

Weizmann, Chaim. *Trial and Error.* New York: Harper & Brothers, 1949.

Wilkie, Katharine E., and Moseley, Elizabeth R. *Kentucky Heritage.* Austin: Steck-Vaughn Company, 1966.

Wilson, Woodrow. *The New Democracy, Presidential Messages, Addresses and Other Papers (1913–1917),* edited by Ray Stannard Baker and William E. Dodd. New York: Harper & Brothers, Publishers, 1926.

Works Progress Administration. *Louisville, A Guide to the Falls City.* American Guide Series. New York: M. Barrows and Company, Incorporated, 1940.

PAMPHLETS AND ARTICLES

Amory, Thomas C. *Old Cambridge and New.* Boston: James R. Osgood & Co., 1871.

Bernard, Burton C. "Brandeis in St. Louis." *St. Louis Bar Journal,* Winter 1964.

Brainin, Joseph. "The Cleveland Drama." *The Jewish Tribune,* July 11, 1930.

Bross, Edgar Clifton. "An Analysis of Louis D. Brandeis." *Eastern and Western Review*, August 1916.

De Haas, Jacob. "The Night in Poreah." *The Jewish Tribune*, February 17, 1928.

Flexner, Bernard. *Mr. Justice Brandeis and the University of Louisville*. Louisville: University of Louisville, 1938.

Freund, Paul A. *Mr. Justice Brandeis: A Centennial Memoir*. Cambridge: The Harvard Law Review Association, 1957.

Hibbard, Caroline I. "Louis D. Brandeis, Advocate of Arbitration." *Strauss Magazine Theatre Program*, March 31, 1913.

Kallen, Horace M. *The Faith of Louis D. Brandeis, Zionist*. New York: Hadassah, n.d.

Levinthal, Louis E. *Louis Dembitz Brandeis*. New York: Zionist Organization of America, 1942.

Rammelkamp, Julian S. "St. Louis in the Early 'Eighties." *The Bulletin* of the Missouri Historical Society, July 1963.

Raushenbush, Paul A. "Starting Unemployment Compensation in Wisconsin." *Unemployment Insurance Review*, April-May, 1967.

Raushenbush, Walter Brandeis. *Brandeis as Jurist: Craftsmanship with Inspiration*. Louisville: University of Louisville School of Law, 1965.

Smythe, William E. "Justice Brandeis in Palestine." *The American Review of Reviews*, June 1919.

Taussig, F. W. "My Father's Business Career." *Harvard Business Review*, Winter 1941.

Tolkowsky, S. *The Jewish Colonization in Palestine*. London: Zionist Organization, n.d.

United States Senate. *Hearings before the Sub-Committee of the Committee on the Judiciary, United States Senate*

. . . *on the Nomination of Louis D. Brandeis to be an Associate Justice of the Supreme Court of the United States.* Washington: The Evening Post Job Printing Office, 1916.

————. *Majority Reports of the Committee on the Judiciary, United States Senate on the Nomination of Hon. Louis D. Brandeis as a Justice of the Supreme Court.* Washington: Government Printing Office, 1916.

Urofsky, Melvin I. "Wilson, Brandeis and the Trust Issue, 1912–1914." *Mid-America,* January 1967.

Voss, Carl Hermann. *Answers on the Palestine Question.* New York: American Christian Palestine Committee, 1947.

Wyatt, Edith. "The New York Cloak-Makers' Strike." *McClure's Magazine,* April 1911.

Index

About the Author

Catherine Owens Peare has always been interested in writing. She was editor of her high school paper, and at New Jersey State Teachers College wrote plays and poetry. After graduation she entered the business world for a while, but her creative ability and interest in education soon led her into writing for young people. This volume is the twenty-seventh in her still growing list of titles. Her *Mahatma Gandhi* received a medal from The Boys Clubs of America, and in 1962 the children of two states chose her biography *The Helen Keller Story* as their favorite, bestowing upon it the William Allen White Award in Kansas and the Sequoyah Award in Oklahoma.

Miss Peare does extensive research for her biographies and feels that travel is essential for authentic results. So far her work has taken her to thirteen foreign countries and to almost every corner of the United States. Her home is in Connecticut.